Composing a Living

Composing a Living

*A Music Creator's Guide to Money,
Relationships, and Business*

Brandon Elliott & Dale Trumbore

OXFORD
UNIVERSITY PRESS

OXFORD
UNIVERSITY PRESS

Oxford University Press is a department of the University of Oxford.
It furthers the University's objective of excellence in research, scholarship,
and education by publishing worldwide. Oxford is a registered trade mark of
Oxford University Press in the UK and in certain other countries.

Published in the United States of America by Oxford University Press
198 Madison Avenue, New York, NY 10016, United States of America.

CIP data is on file at the Library of Congress

ISBN 9780197803479 (pbk.)
ISBN 9780197803462 (hbk.)

DOI: 10.1093/9780197803509.001.0001

Paperback printed by Sheridan Books, Inc., United States of America
Hardback printed by Lightning Source, Inc., United States of America

The manufacturer's authorized representative in the EU for product safety is
Oxford University Press España S.A., Parque Empresarial San Fernando de Henares,
Avenida de Castilla, 2 – 28830 Madrid (www.oup.es/en or product.safety@oup.com).
OUP España S.A. also acts as importer into Spain of products made by the manufacturer.

Dedicated to Dale Warland, our mentor and friend.

Note to the Reader

The information presented herein represents the view of the authors as of the date of publication and is presented for informational purposes only. It should not be construed as legal, accounting, or professional advice. The opinions expressed are solely those of the authors or the interviewed composers and may evolve based on new information or changing circumstances.

The majority of the legal opinions and descriptions of financial entities pertain specifically to laws in the United States. While much advice shared here is applicable to readers in any country, readers outside the United States should consult their own financial advisors and relevant laws to determine the financial and legal options for their country.

While the authors have made every effort to ensure the accuracy and completeness of the information contained herein, neither the authors nor their affiliated partners assume any responsibility for any errors, inaccuracies, or omissions. Additionally, all interviews featured here were conducted voluntarily. The views, thoughts, and opinions expressed by those interviewed composers are their own and do not necessarily represent those of the authors.

Contents

Biographies of Composers Interviewed

This book features quotes from the following composers. For the sake of readability, their biographies are listed here, rather than throughout the book. Read the biographies now, or refer back to them as composers are featured in the book.

Julia Adolphe's music is described as "alive with invention" (*New Yorker*), "colorful, mercurial, deftly orchestrated" (*New York Times*), and displaying "a remarkable gift for sustaining a compelling musical narrative" (*Musical America*). Adolphe's works are performed internationally by renowned ensembles such as the New York Philharmonic, Los Angeles Philharmonic, Boston Symphony, Cincinnati Symphony, Gewandhausorchester Leipzig, LA Chamber Orchestra, and Chamber Music Society of Lincoln Center, among others. Passionate about de-stigmatizing mental illness and sharing tools to cultivate a healthier, sustainable relationship with one's artistic process, Adolphe is the creator and host of the podcast *LooseLeaf NoteBook*, produced in partnership with New Music USA.

Three-time Grammy-nominated American composer **Miguel del Águila** creates distinctive, innovative modern classical music highly influenced by his Latin American roots. With sixty-four CDs released, his music enjoys over two hundred live performances yearly, earning acclaim like "brilliant and witty" (*New York Times*) and "sonically dazzling" (*Los Angeles Times*). Thousands of first-rate artists have performed his music worldwide, including over a hundred orchestras led by conductors such as Leonard Slatkin, Lukas Foss, JoAnn Falletta, Giancarlo Guerrero, Marin Alsop, and Carlos Miguel Prieto. He has received a Kennedy Center Friedheim Award, New Music USA's Music Alive and Magnum Opus awards, and a Copland Foundation award, among many others.

Juhi Bansal is an Indian-born, Hong Kong–raised composer known for her "radiant and transcendent" music (*New Classic LA*) and her "management of color and light" (*Washington Post*). Drawing upon a tapestry of influences, her music weaves together themes of cultural diversity, environment, and women-centered narratives. Awarded by the Barlow Endowment, Opera America, ASCAP, Cantori New York, and with music on several Grammy-nominated albums, her work creates immersive musical experiences that ask audiences to rethink what they know, examine the unfamiliar, and consider what we can do to create positive change.

Five-time Emmy Award–winner **Jeff Beal**'s improvisatory method, sense of timing, and sophistication have made him a favorite of directors including Ed Harris (*Pollock* and *Appaloosa*), David Fincher (*House of Cards*), and Oliver Stone (*JFK Revisited*, *The Putin Interviews*). Inventive scores for HBO's *Rome*, *Carnivàle*, *The Newsroom*, USA's *Monk*, Netflix's *House of Cards*, *The Queen of Versailles*, and *Blackfish* have shown him to be one of the most distinctive and recognizable composers working today. Beal is also a prolific composer and conductor of concert music, with premieres by the St. Louis Symphony Orchestra, the Los Angeles Master Chorale, and Smuin Ballet. In 2016, Beal and his wife Joan endowed the Beal Institute for Film Music and Contemporary Media at their alma mater the Eastman School of Music.

Composer **Abbie Betinis** creates "inventive" (*New York Times*), "joyful . . . incandescent" (*Boston Globe*) and "beguiling" (*BBC Music Magazine*) music. With performances from Carnegie Hall to Disney Hall, state prisons to capitol buildings, international cathedrals to intimate summer campfires, her music transports performers and audiences alike through storytelling, relevance, and craft. A two-time McKnight Artist Fellow, and recognized by *Musical America* for her "ability to use her talents to effect social change," she is coeditor of the *Justice Choir Songbook*—a resource for community transformation through singing. She lives in Minnesota, where she has taught composition at Concordia University–St. Paul and St. Olaf College.

Saunder Choi, a Filipino composer and choral artist based in Los Angeles, has earned international acclaim with performances by groups like Conspirare, Philippine Madrigal Singers, and the Los Angeles Master Chorale. He has arranged for Lea Salonga, the San Francisco Gay Men's Chorus, San Francisco Symphony, and many others. He sings with Pacific Chorale, L.A. Choral Lab, and HEX Vocal Ensemble, as well as in film scores like Disney's *The Lion King*, *Mulan*, *Avatar 2*, and others. His compositions champion DEIJ themes, including immigration, racial justice, LGBTQ+ advocacy, climate justice, and representations of his Filipino-Chinese heritage.

Philadelphia-based composer **Melissa Dunphy** specializes in vocal, political, and theatrical music. Her commissions include choral works for VOCES 8, Cantus, the BBC Singers, the King's Singers, and Chor Leoni, and the opera *Alice Tierney* for Oberlin Conservatory. She is also a Barrymore Award–nominated theater composer and has served as Director of Music Composition for the O'Neill National Puppetry Conference. Dunphy has a PhD in composition from the University of Pennsylvania and a BM from West Chester University, and she teaches at Rutgers University. Along with her husband, Matt, she hosts the podcast *The Boghouse* about the couple's adventures in Philadelphia colonial archaeology.

Reena Esmail works between the worlds of Indian and Western classical music, and brings communities together through the creation of equitable musical spaces. Esmail holds degrees from the Juilliard School and the Yale School of Music. A resident of Los Angeles, Esmail is the '20–25 Swan Family Artist in Residence with Los Angeles Master Chorale, and was the '20–21 Composer in Residence with Seattle Symphony. She is a Cofounder and Artistic Director of Shastra, a nonprofit organization that promotes cross-cultural music connecting musical traditions of India and the West.

Sydney Guillaume is a distinguished Haitian-American composer and conductor celebrated for his intricate choral and instrumental works that blend Haitian culture with concert music. Praised by the *Miami Herald* for their "impressive maturity and striking melodic distinction," Guillaume's compositions have been commissioned and performed by renowned choirs such as Seraphic Fire, the Westminster Chorus, the University of Miami Frost Chorale, the Nathaniel Dett Chorale, the Saint Louis Chamber Singers, and the Miami Children's Chorus. Guillaume leads workshops at universities and high schools throughout North America, conducts regional and national honor choirs, and self-publishes nearly all of his compositions.

Jocelyn Hagen composes music that has been described as "simply magical" (*Fanfare Magazine*) and "dramatic and deeply moving" (*Star Tribune*, Minneapolis/St. Paul). She is a pioneer in the field of composition, pushing the expectations of musicians and audiences with large-scale multimedia works, electro-acoustic music, dance, and opera. Her melodic music is rhythmically driven and texturally complex, rich in color, and deeply heartfelt. A champion of the female spirit, many of her projects focus on the stories of women. She is a cofounder of Graphite Publishing and the band Nation, singing her heart out every chance she gets.

Jennifer Jolley is a composer, conductor, and professor. Addressing a range of topics such as climate change, #MeToo, feminist history, and the abuses of the Putin regime, Jennifer strives to write pieces that are equally enjoyable and meaningful. Jennifer's works have been commissioned and performed by ensembles worldwide, including the US Navy Band, Vermont Symphony Orchestra, Left Coast Chamber Ensemble, and Quince Ensemble. Her music has been featured in venues such as Carnegie Hall, the Rivera Court at the Detroit Institute of Arts, Žofín Palace, and Namhansanseong Art Hall. In 2023, she was a Fulbright Scholar to Egypt.

Molly Joyce has been deemed one of the "most versatile, prolific and intriguing composers working under the vast new-music dome" by the *Washington Post*. Her music has additionally been described as "serene power" (*New York Times*) and "unwavering . . . enveloping" (*Vulture*). Her work is concerned with disability as a creative source. She has an impaired left hand from a previous car accident, and seeks to explore disability through composition, performance, collaboration, community engagement, and further mediums.

Shawn Kirchner is a composer/arranger, singer, and pianist based in Los Angeles whose long creative association with the Los Angeles Master Chorale culminated in his tenure as the ensemble's Composer in Residence from 2012 to 2015. Kirchner's music, which bridges classical and folk traditions, has made its way throughout the world, championed by leading choirs and publishers. His original songwriting ranges in style from jazz to gospel to bluegrass, with the latter featured on his *Meet Me on the Mountain* recording. Kirchner's composing is also informed by his work as a professional chorister, feature film session singer, and church musician.

Thomas Kotcheff is a Los Angeles–based composer and pianist. His concert music has been performed internationally by the Riot Ensemble, Seattle Symphony, New York Youth Symphony, wild Up, Sandbox Percussion, Alinde Quartett, and the Aspen Contemporary Ensemble. Thomas composes and orchestrates music for film, television, and digital media. His film credits include *Oppenheimer*, *Black Panther: Wakanda Forever*, and *The Wild Robot*, among others. As a pianist, Thomas has dedicated himself to commissioning and premiering new piano works. He is the founding member of the Los Angeles–based piano duo HOCKET and is a Core Artist with Piano Spheres.

Morten Johannes Lauridsen was awarded the 2007 National Medal of Arts, the highest artistic award in the United States, by the President in a White House ceremony "for his composition of radiant choral works combining musical beauty, power, and spiritual depth that have thrilled audiences worldwide." He taught at the USC Thornton School of Music for over fifty years where he chaired the Department of Composition and founded the Advanced Studies Program in Film Scoring. His works are recorded on hundreds of CDs, several of which received Grammy nominations. In 2016, Mr. Lauridsen received the ASCAP Foundation "Life in Music" Award.

Angélica Negrón is a Puerto Rican–born composer and multi-instrumentalist. She writes music for voices, orchestras, and film as well as robots, toys, and plants. Angélica is known for playing with the unexpected intersection of classical and electronic music, unusual instruments, and found sounds. Recent commissions include works for the Los Angeles Philharmonic, New York Philharmonic, New York Botanical Garden, and Kronos Quartet. She regularly performs a solo show and is a founding member of the tropical electronic band Balún. Angélica lives in Brooklyn, always looking for ways to incorporate her love of drag, comedy, and the natural world into her work.

Shara Nova has released six chamber-pop albums under the moniker My Brightest Diamond. She has composed works for ensembles such as the Crossing, Conspirare, Roomful of Teeth, the Detroit Opera's educational touring company, yMusic, Oregon Symphony, Indianapolis Symphony, American Composers Orchestra, and BBC Concert Orchestra. She was an original member of the Broadway show *Illinoise*, and her album *The Blue Hour* (Nonesuch Records) was included in NPR's Top 10 Albums of 2022. Nova is a three-time Grammy nominee, an Opera America Discovery Grant awardee, a Carolina Performing Arts Creative Futures fellow, and a United States Artists fellow.

Dr. Zanaida Stewart Robles is an award-winning Black American female composer, vocalist, and teacher. Authentic interpersonal connection and relationship building are core principles of her teaching and performance methods. Born, raised, and educated in Southern California, living on the unceded lands of the Tongva-Gabrielino peoples, she is in demand as a composer, vocalist, clinician, and adjudicator. Dr. Robles's compositions are published and have been studied and performed by professional ensembles, educational institutions, churches, and individuals worldwide. Dr. Robles holds a DMA degree from the USC Thornton School of Music, an MM degree from CSU Northridge, and a BM degree from CSU Long Beach.

Considered "one of the best of the younger American composers" (*Chicago Tribune*), Emmy-winning and Grammy-nominated composer and conductor

Jake Runestad has received commissions and performances from leading ensembles worldwide. Dubbed a "choral rockstar" by American Public Media, Jake creates thoughtful and compelling works "that speak to some of the most pressing and moving issues of our time" (*Star Tribune*). His visceral music and charismatic personality have fostered a busy schedule of commissions, residencies, workshops, and conducting engagements, enabling him to share his passion for creativity, expressivity, and community with musicians around the globe.

Isaac Io Schankler (they/them) is a composer, accordionist, and electronic musician based in southern California. Their music has been described as "beautiful, algorithmic, organic, dystopian" (*I Care If You Listen*) and "remarkable listening" (*Sequenza21*). They have collaborated with a variety of ensembles, including the Ray-Kallay Duo, Friction Quartet, C3LA, SPLICE Ensemble, Autoduplicity, Nouveau Classical Project, and Los Angeles Percussion Quartet. Additionally, Schankler has written music for acclaimed video games like *Ladykiller in a Bind* and *Depression Quest*. Schankler is artistic director of concert series People Inside Electronics and Associate Professor of Music at Cal Poly Pomona.

Alex Shapiro has built an unconventional life interweaving her dynamic musical career with avid pursuits of wildlife photography, nonfiction writing, and a devotion to advocacy. Her works are heard daily in concerts and broadcasts and can be found on over forty commercially released recordings from around the world. Ms. Shapiro holds the Symphonic & Concert writer member seat on the Board of Directors of ASCAP and also serves on the boards of the ASCAP Foundation, the Aaron Copland Fund for Music, and the Music Publishers Association of the United States, representing her company, Activist Music LLC.

Derrick Skye is a Los Angeles–based composer and musician celebrated for his transcultural approach to music, blending global traditions with Western classical practices. The *Los Angeles Times* praised his music as "something to savor," while *The Times* (London) called it "deliciously head-spinning." His work has been commissioned and performed by prestigious ensembles like the BBC National Orchestra of Wales, Los Angeles Philharmonic, London Philharmonic, and Los Angeles Chamber Orchestra. Skye is Artistic Director of Bridge to Everywhere and serves on the boards of American Composers Forum and New Music USA. His music fosters cultural understanding and connection through collaboration.

The music of **Kile Smith** has received three Grammy nominations and is hailed for its strong voice, sheer beauty, and "profoundly direct emotional appeal." Craig Hella Johnson calls Kile "one of our most important composers . . . his voice is unlike any other. Utterly unique." Commissioned multiple times by the Crossing and Conspirare, and by many of the nation's top professional and university choirs, he is regularly performed nationally and internationally. His *Vespers* was called "spectacular" (*Gramophone*), "a major new work" (*American Record Guide*), and "a masterpiece of the deepest kind . . . easily one of the best releases of the year of any type" (*Audiophile Audition*).

Inspired by narrative, magical realism, speculative fiction, and making better humans through art, the music of **Timothy C. Takach** is a mainstay in the concert world. Applauded for his melodic lines, text choices, and rich, intriguing harmonies, his compositions are performed worldwide. He is a co-founder of Cantus, Graphite Publishing, and Nation, and he is a co-creator of the theatrical production *All Is Calm: the Christmas Truce of 1914*. Takach has frequent work as a composer-in-residence, presenter, conductor, clinician, and lecturer.

Dara Taylor has emerged as a fresh voice in the world of scoring, as evidenced by her score to Amazon Studios' film *The Tender Bar*, directed by Academy Award–winning filmmaker George Clooney, and Universal Pictures' *Strays*, starring Will Ferrell and Jamie Foxx. Her other credits include Sony Pictures' *The Invitation*, for which she received a 2023 SCL Award Nomination; Netflix's *The Noel Diary*, directed by Academy Award–nominated filmmaker Charles Shyer; Lionsgate's *Barb and Star Go to Vista del Mar*, starring Kristen Wiig; and the Karen Allen–starred drama *Colewell*, for which she won a 2019 Hollywood Music in Media award.

Composer **Frank Ticheli**'s music has been described as being "optimistic and thoughtful" (*Los Angeles Times*), "lean and muscular" (*New York Times*), and "powerful, deeply felt crafted with impressive flair and an ear for striking instrumental colors" (*South Florida Sun-Sentinel*). Ticheli is Professor Emeritus at the University of Southern California's Thornton School of Music, where he taught for thirty-two years. His orchestral works have received considerable recognition in the United States and Europe, with performances by the orchestras of Philadelphia, Atlanta, Detroit, Dallas, Nashville, Stuttgart, Frankfurt, and many others. He is best known, however, for his works for wind ensemble and concert band, many of which have become standards in the repertoire.

Award-winning transgender Mexican-American composer, native of North Texas, **Mari Esabel Valverde**, whose music has been reviewed as "heart-stopping" (*BBC Music Magazine*) and "of shimmering beauty" (*The WholeNote*), has composed art songs, chamber music, and works for chorus, orchestra, and wind ensemble. Recent projects include commissions for the Gay and Lesbian Association of Choruses, Los Angeles Master Chorale, and the University of Michigan Men's Glee Club. Aspiring to create music that emboldens people to unlearn shame, her works center the voices of historically marginalized authors and address questions of gender, sexuality, social justice, and love of the natural world.

Grammy Award–winning composer and conductor **Eric Whitacre** is among today's most popular musicians. A graduate of the Juilliard School, his works are programmed worldwide and his groundbreaking Virtual Choirs have united well over 100,000 singers from more than 145 countries. A charismatic speaker, he has given keynote addresses for Apple, Google, World Economic Forum, United Nations Speakers Program, and the mainstage TED conference. Eric Whitacre has written for and conducted many of the world's leading choirs and orchestras and performs regularly at Carnegie Hall, the Royal Albert Hall, and Sydney Opera House.

Introduction

Composing a Career

Our desire to write this book was motivated by one dangerous sentence. It has the single-handed power to derail an entire composition career, and most composers have heard it at least once. Maybe you've heard a parent say it, or your music theory professor, or your grandma who still wants you to become a lawyer. That sentence? *You can't make a living writing music.*

If you've caught yourself believing this lie, you are not alone. Even some professional musicians still believe that composers can't make a living writing music. While the journey is hard, it is far from impossible. Many composers have made the leap from composing for free to composing for money. Some of these composers make a substantial, livable wage from their creative efforts.

While making a living writing music is possible, it isn't easy, nor is it a typical forty-hour-per-week day job. However, by thoughtfully honing your skills and managing your craft as a business, you can orchestrate your own full-time living as a composer. More than half of the twenty-eight composers interviewed for this book make the bulk of their living from composing, and the others integrate teaching and/or performing into their income. These successful composers aren't mythical creatures; they're real human beings, and there are many more of them beyond the creatives we've spoken to here. The myth that "you can't make a living writing music" has to end.

So how *do* you make a living in music?

- At the start of your career, you assess your skills, strengths, and resources, the topic of Chapter 1.
- You nurture relationships with other musicians whose work you respect, the topic of Chapter 2.
- You cultivate a successful mindset around money and business, the topic of Chapter 3.
- You create goals that merge strategy with foundational economic principles, the topic of Chapter 4.

Composing a Living. Brandon Elliott and Dale Trumbore, Oxford University Press.
© Brandon Elliott and Dale Trumbore 2025. DOI: 10.1093/9780197803509.003.0001

- You establish a strong foundation for your career by improving your craft, purchasing equipment you will actually use, and creating strong recordings, the topic of Chapter 5.
- You learn how to value and price your work effectively, the topic of Chapter 6.
- You build a diverse portfolio of active and passive income streams based on your strengths as a musician, the topic of Chapter 7.
- When you need assistance with your workflow, you assemble a helpful team around you, the topic of Chapter 8.
- You evaluate whether transitioning to a full-time freelance career is right for you, and if it is, you make that leap slowly and carefully, the topic of Chapter 9.
- You learn to "think like a lawyer" when navigating contracts, copyright, and other legal matters, the topic of Chapter 10.
- You learn basic accounting and other financial principles, then ask whether incorporating is the right step for your business, the topic of Chapter 11.
- You set and plan for long-term financial goals, the topic of Chapter 12.
- Above all, you embrace the dual role of artist and entrepreneur, ensuring that your creative vision is supported by sound business practices and thoughtful career planning.

If you are anything like us—your coauthors, Brandon Elliott and Dale Trumbore—you may have found the existing resources on making a living as a composer somewhat lacking. Trumbore is a composer and writer who has built a freelance composing career from scratch, with helpful advice along the way from friends and mentors. She has long wished she could read a single book for composers on how to make a living in this business. Elliott is a conductor, consultant, and professor who has taught music business courses for nearly a decade. In his experience, while there are plenty of books that offer a great panoramic view of the music industry as a whole, these books are primarily focused on the pop and rock music industry. (Moving forward, we'll be referring to ourselves in the third person when we want to share a personal anecdote.)

There is a lack of resources to guide composers of concert music on how to integrate practical advice on music business into their lives. This book is an attempt to fill that void with an evergreen resource for early- and mid-career composers. Since so many concert music composers share an interest in film and video game scoring, this book also notes how building a sustainable career in concert music does or does not overlap with best practices to carve out a career in that industry. The principles discussed here—particularly with regard to financial and legal matters—pertain primarily to the United States. Still, many of the principles discussed here will be relevant to composers of other genres, composers based outside the United States, and musicians as a whole.

As you read, you will see references to the Resources section at the end of the book. This section includes recommended further reading; online business, financial, and legal tools; and other suggestions that can aid you on your composing journey. The more resources you have, the easier it will be for you to carve out a sustainable composing career. You'll also notice that several ideas in this book will return time and again, as many of the principles, resources, and examples given are interconnected.

Your ultimate goal might be to make the jump to full-time music composition, or you may hope to merge another job—teaching, performing, arts administration, or a career outside of music—with composition. Regardless of your career goals, you will be well served by the principles discussed in this book: building collaborative relationships, assessing your portfolio of skills, cultivating diverse income streams, and understanding financial and music business principles well enough to put them into practice. You'll also read quotes and anecdotes offering twenty-eight composers' perspectives on what it takes to succeed as a composer, as well as prompts encouraging you to recognize whether making a living writing music is the best way to have the compositional life you want.

Because each new stage of a composing career is accompanied by unprecedented obstacles, many composers feel as though they never truly have everything "figured out." The good news? If you are a composer, you already know what it's like to have to begin over and over. With every new piece you write, you start at the beginning, knowing that the journey ahead might be a treacherous one. When you encounter and solve musical dilemmas, your composing skills level up. Yes, you face new challenges in each new piece you write, but your overall problem-solving abilities are constantly improving.

Building a sustainable career in composition draws on the same problem-solving skills. This book shares a wealth of practical information paired with real-world examples: mistakes that other composers have made so you don't have to, as well as best practices to light your path ahead. There are some decisions that only you can make for yourself, like what pricing methods to use for your work or whether a freelance career is right for you. In those cases, you'll read examples of how other composers have forged their own trails, along with decision-making guidance to help you.

The interviews for this project included questions rooted in money and business practices that you'll find answered in the following chapters:

- "Do you believe you can build a career as a musician with zero dollars to your name?"
- "What is one thing related to making money as a musician that you learned later in life but wish you knew when starting your professional career?"
- "What is the best financial decision you've made so far?"
- "How have you approached goal-setting in your career?"
- "Have your goals and your approach to goal-setting changed over time?"
- "What do you think constitutes success as a composer?"
- "Do you feel that you've 'made it'?"

Many composers feel as if they're not "successful" enough, but what exactly does it mean to succeed in composition? While you'll read several perspectives on making it as a composer, only you can answer how you define achievement. For composers who span multiple genres—concert music, jazz, film or video game scores, electronic music, and more—and for those who combine composing with other jobs, this definition becomes even more individualized. Your definition of success will likely evolve over time. When you do define success for yourself, hold that definition loosely; you'll likely rewrite it several times over the course of your career.

Music is rooted in community. In the interviews conducted for this book, it didn't matter whether composers were discussing money, business, goal setting, or success; conversations always turned to the importance of forming strong relationships. Many of the composers interviewed said that collaborations with friends—which often began with no money exchanged—have generated some of their most fulfilling and long-lasting working relationships. For other composers, a single influential mentor's encouragement was enough to kick-start their entire creative career. The financial success of your music career revolves around the people you meet and the connections you foster. You'll find these relationships to be just as important to your thriving professional career as the money you make and the music you create.

If you can marry craft and dedication to relationship building and solid business principles, you'll have what it takes to succeed as a composer. If you are willing to put in the work to "make it" in this career, you can find success in music, whether that means full-time composing or writing music alongside other work. Don't stop before you've given yourself a chance to get started. You *can* make a living as a composer. Here's how.

1

Starting to Start

Composers arrive at the field of writing music with vastly different levels of knowledge, skills, and resources, including a wide array of financial backgrounds. Many professional musicians receive years of costly lessons in their early childhood, and the lack of such a background—or a late start to a music career—can be daunting for anyone contemplating a career in music. In recent decades, though, the barrier to entry for a career in composition has lowered, thanks to the emergence of music notation software, digital audio workstations (DAWs), and online tutorials. Now, it is more possible than ever to teach yourself the skills needed to thrive as a composer, no matter your financial background.

Composer Juhi Bansal acknowledges that if you are starting from close to nothing in the way of financial resources, though, breaking into a composition career can be daunting. "You will find it's not impossible, but you will find it extremely, extremely challenging and exponentially harder than your colleagues, in a field that's already really hard to break into," she says. However, if you have good connections and relationships, "that can make up for a whole lot of what you don't necessarily have in funding."

When we asked composers what they wished they had known when they were first starting out, many echoed Bansal's advice, citing the early importance of building significant relationships with collaborators. Other composers discussed ways they wished they had invested money in their careers, pursued opportunities that allowed them to improve their craft, or built a professional portfolio. Some wished they had prioritized paying down or avoiding debt earlier in their careers. Ultimately, our interviews revealed four main factors that most composers found essential to the start of their own careers:

- Honing your craft
- Building your musical community
- Identifying the resources you already have at hand
- Establishing "safety nets" through non-composing work

Composing a Living. Brandon Elliott and Dale Trumbore, Oxford University Press.
© Brandon Elliott and Dale Trumbore 2025. DOI: 10.1093/9780197803509.003.0002

Whether you're starting with limited resources or building on a solid foundation, embracing these strategies can pave the way for growth and fulfillment. By thoughtfully integrating them into your craft, you create a career aligned with your passion. In this way, advancing your skills becomes both the means and the reward of your artistic journey.

Honing Your Craft

The most important factor that you can control early on in your career is strengthening your ability to write music. Honing your craft can take a variety of forms discussed below:

- Learning to engrave your scores cleanly, notating them in an accessible and logical way
- "Iterating" through experimentation: write a variety of music for different kinds of ensembles and instruments, to hone your creative voice, discover personal preferences, and gain as much composing experience as possible
- Writing for an ensemble in which you are also a performer, to become fluent in the nuances of that specific art form
- Becoming proficient in using a digital audio workstation (DAW) and other relevant software, if you are interested in composing for electronic media

Zanaida Stewart Robles regrets waiting until there was already a demand for her work before she invested hours learning how to cleanly notate her scores. "It doesn't matter how wonderful your musical ideas are if you can't deliver [a score] on time and notate it in a way that people can read it," she says. "It's not intuitive for some of us, and those are practical skills that you can be practicing and honing as your career develops and grows." She urges beginning composers to develop their craft even if no one is commissioning them. If Robles could go back in time, she would spend her earliest days as a composer developing a composition practice. That could have included writing a melody a day or composing for a set number of minutes, she says—something to help her "musical chops stay fresh" and to feed her musical soul.

Many composers recommend taking on as much composing work as your schedule will allow at the start of your career. Your composing time may be limited if, for example, you are a student, you are the primary childcare provider in your household, you have a chronic health issue, or you have a part- or full-time job in another field. As you are starting out, though, gaining as much composing experience as your schedule allows will refine your voice and reveal the kind of creative work you most enjoy.

One way to develop your craft quickly is to start or join an ensemble and then compose for it. You'll receive real-time feedback and recognize what music truly serves (or doesn't serve) the ensemble's needs. In many ensembles, you'll also meet musicians who teach or conduct in addition to performing, who may also be eager to perform your work or use it with their students. Taking on a part-time job in music, such as a paid performing gig, can also create opportunities for connections and commissions while providing you with essential income.

For Saunder Choi, being part of the Philippine Madrigal Singers was a crucial part of his development as a composer. As a singer, arranger, and composer for the group, Choi had a chance to hone his compositional craft and form relationships with other singers, composers, and conductors. His compositional efforts paid off, as the music he wrote for the ensemble has been performed multiple times, including internationally. "Writing for them was such a rewarding experience," he says. "I still reap those benefits today, years after leaving the group."

If you compose for film, honing your craft requires a slightly different perspective. "Step one is making sure that you are familiar with a sequencer and a DAW [digital audio workstation], not just pen and paper [and] not just Sibelius or Finale," Dara Taylor says. "Step two is learning to be a little less precious with every note," because film composition moves at a much faster pace than writing concert music. Beyond that, she says, "start scoring any film you can find: student films, low-budget indie things. There are lots of indie film festivals and places to talk to directors."

Film composers Jeff Beal and Thomas Kotcheff both emphasize the importance of credits for early-career film composers. This is particularly true when you are working with or ghostwriting for a collaborator, as film composers often start out working for other composers. Because the pay for entry-level jobs can be low—these jobs may be viewed as stepping stones to future work and résumé building, rather than a high source of income—look for the nonmonetary value of receiving writing credits for your work.

Building Community from Scratch

Composing can be a lonely pursuit. Apart from attending rehearsals and premieres, you may often find yourself working solo. If you are isolated from other composers, you'll have few chances to take stock of your own career in conjunction with that of your peers—to ask yourself where you belong and seek advice from those who may already have overcome the struggles you are facing. Without a community, it can be hard to know whether you are on the right path. Unless you are writing music for only yourself to hear, you are going to need performers, conductors, listeners, fans, and other collaborators. How do you find them?

Building Community in Concert Music

Between K–12 schools, colleges, churches, and community groups, most composers live within driving distance of at least one ensemble. Within those local ensembles, you'll find soloists: a paid singer within a church choir, for example, or a first-chair high school violinist. Concert composers can start building a musical network by asking how to best serve their community of soloists and ensembles. This approach requires you to adopt an entrepreneurial mindset, but also an attitude of empathy. Who is your audience, and what do they need? How does the music they need differ from or overlap with the music you want to create?

If you can fill a gap in your community—writing music that serves young musicians or community ensembles, for example, or music that communicates a unique message—you may also identify a larger need that no one else has addressed. In this way, finding performers and commissioners for your work becomes an act of service. Instead of approaching collaborators with the mindset of "Here's my music, and I want you to perform it," you are asking: "What are your unique needs, and how can I write something to fill those needs in a creative way?"

If you have studied an instrument, you already have a sense of the repertoire that you do or don't like to play. You have a sense of how other composers write for your instrument, and you know what you love in certain pieces and loathe in others. Above all, you have a sense of the gaps in that repertoire. If you are unsatisfied with elements of the music written for your instrument, you are probably not the only one who feels that way. You can fill in those gaps and serve your musical community by writing music that's compelling to practice and perform.

A few years ago, a friend of Brandon Elliott's asked for advice on starting a professional composition career. Elliott urged that friend to write down a list of twenty conductors the friend knew well, then put a star next to five that they were pretty sure would agree to commission them today, even if that commission was only for a hundred dollars. The friend followed up on those connections and received five commissions that first year. Granted, the commissions ranged from a hundred to several hundred dollars each, but Elliott's friend went from zero composing income to generating over a thousand dollars in a week, simply by starting with whom he knew already. Starting at the beginning often means asking yourself whom you already know.

"I think the best thing I've done for my career is going to St. Olaf and making all the relationships that I have there, writing a lot of music in that time, loving myself, and beginning my [gender] transition," Mari Esabel Valverde says. For Valverde, choosing a specific academic environment led to numerous musical friendships, a strong sense of her personal identity, and the development of her craft. Despite taking on student loans to attend St. Olaf, she calls it "the best decision."

Composition students have a built-in advantage when it comes to finding and building a music community. Within a music school or department, composers can meet other musicians in shared classes, participate in ensembles with conductors and performers who may later program or commission their music, and encounter professors and other mentors who can offer helpful craft and career advice. If you didn't attend music school, though, or if you graduated long ago, you can still continue growing your community at music conferences, through social media or other online communities, or through joining an ensemble.

Building Community in Multimedia Composition

Dara Taylor and Jeff Beal agree that in film composition, it's not only directors with whom you want to form relationships: it's everyone involved in the production of a film. "A lot of times people think you just go straight to the director," Taylor says, "but there are so many different ways that people get jobs. Getting to know editors is helpful, especially in the [independent film] world, because a lot of times they are the ones that are putting temp music into a film." Beal agrees, noting that since editors and composers tend to work very closely together, if you are friends with an editor and they like your music, they're more likely to use your music in the "temp track"—a temporary score made up of existing music that serves as a placeholder, using music similar to the score that will eventually make up the actual soundtrack. If a director likes your music for the temp track, this logic goes, they may want to collaborate with you on a real score.

Taylor has been recommended for projects by people from all departments, she says, including assistants, editors, directors of photography, and cinematographers. This kind of networking sounds intimidating until you realize that it's a collaborative business, as Taylor says, and people are usually eager to get to know other people. "Don't be afraid to ask for help," she urges. "Creating those relationships and making those friends is helpful." Taylor has been working with the same guitarist for ten years. Whereas at the start of her career, she may have paid that guitarist in pizza to play for a short film, now she can afford the going rate to have them record a feature. "Don't expect to be an island and to have to do everything by yourself," she says, noting that this outlook—a composer playing and orchestrating on their own—is sometimes unhealthily romanticized in the film world. Realistically, Taylor says, "that sounds miserable." She notes that one of her favorite parts of her career is getting to work with other people.

Like Taylor, Isaac Io Schankler recommends cultivating a "supportive community where everyone is sharing resources and helping each other out." Schankler, who has scored several independent video games, found early success sharing their work and engaging in new-music communities on social media, particularly Twitter. That specific path, however, is already out of date. Instead, Schankler suggests that the timeless lesson from their experience may be to seek out and join smaller, self-selecting communities where there is a culture of sharing work and resources.

Even composers who primarily work alone still need collaborators. Build your composing career by cultivating working relationships and friendships with other musicians. Strengthen and add value to your community by recommending and sharing others' music, meeting like-minded musicians through an ensemble or music school, or asking the musicians you already know to introduce you to other composers and performers. (The importance of relationship building to a composing career will be discussed in greater detail in the following chapter.)

Identifying Skill Sets and Resources

"If I would have known early on how many different ways that a composer could make money," Derrick Skye says, "I would have been able to act on getting to those ways a lot sooner." When you are embarking on a composing career, it's never too early to identify what makes you unique. Are you a performer as well as a composer? Do you have strong writing and/or grant-writing skills? Do you know how to code as well as compose? Most composers interviewed here have at least one side skill that enhances their ability to work as a composer.

Dale Trumbore is fond of asking the following question whenever she's talking to a composer, emerging or established, who feels stuck in their career: *What can you create right now, with your current resources?* Your resources could include musical skills—composing, engineering, performing, conducting, or producing—or non-musical talents, like cooking, gardening, graphic design, or photography. Perhaps you could compose an entire album for yourself to record, or you could produce an album for a friend, gaining valuable editing and production experience in the process. You can always write music for colleagues who are performers, but you may have other creative acquaintances, too. Maybe you know a choreographer, filmmaker, poet, programmer, video-game developer, or visual artist who would love to collaborate.

Safety Nets and Day Jobs

Some composers start their careers with quite a few resources. They have "safety nets" in the form of family support, spousal income, or access to healthcare, or monetary income in the form of investments or other assets. However, as Abbie Betinis points out, you can view many different kinds of assets and skills as alternate forms of "safety nets" within a composition career. These factors can be just as valuable as strictly financial assets. Betinis names the following as examples of "safety nets"—skills beyond financial resources that can enable a thriving composing career:

- A world-class education
- Writing or speaking skills
- Living in an area with ample grants for the kind of music you create
- Grant-writing skills
- A cooperative living arrangement
- Ability to barter skills or goods with friends
- Financial savvy
- An aptitude for relationship building

"It should probably be said out loud that starting from zero is a dream for a lot of people," Betinis says, "because a lot of us start with a lot of debt." The composers interviewed here largely agreed that it's virtually impossible to build a career if you're starting with zero dollars to your name. But any combination of financial resources, connections with potential collaborators, or the skill sets Betinis mentions above can set you up for success in this field.

A part- or full-time job alongside composition can be another kind of safety net. As you begin your composing career, you may need to take on any work you can find in order to meet your basic needs. That money will likely come from sources outside of the music field, and that's okay. In fact, that's more than okay: it's common, practical, and realistic. Many composers ensure their early financial stability with day jobs or side jobs outside of music.

Dara Taylor encourages beginning composers to take on work beyond composition, at least at the start of their careers. "Don't be afraid to take a job, whether that's working for another composer or teaching" or another job, she says. "Don't expect this to be your main source of income, because it won't be for a while. So have [another] job, and then you'll feel the flexibility to be able to take on a [composing] project that might be really rewarding creatively, but not so rewarding monetarily."

If you do take on a part- or full-time job alongside your composing, consider work that still allows you time to compose. Jocelyn Hagen suggests that you avoid a job that "sucks your soul." She says, "In terms of your art and your artistry, you have to find something that is also fun without a lot of pressure. If you get sucked into a job where [that job is] all you think about and all you can do, or it's a toxic work environment, that will swallow up your whole life." After college, Hagen enjoyed holding a part-time job as a bank teller. "That was great because it taught me about money. It was kind of mindless, and I could get health insurance working only twenty, twenty-five hours a week." In an ideal situation, when you are starting out, your priority will be not just taking *any* job, but a part- or full-time job that also allows you the time and presence of mind to continue honing your composing skills.

For many composers, honing one's craft and believing in oneself are essential steps in a thriving professional career. But for those elements to translate into opportunities, there's an important next move: cultivating relationships with peers, collaborators, mentors, and fans.

2

Building Relationships

Many composers regard their professional networks as a system of genuine friendships. The relationships may involve mutually beneficial transactions, but they are also built on warmth and a strong sense of community. Jake Runestad says he views his "musical family" as a garden:

> I nurture these relationships in hopes that they will "bear fruit." This isn't a superficial attempt at throwing my music at people and seeing what sticks; rather, it's an intentional investment in relationships that bring meaning to our collective lives (which may blossom into the professional things a composer hopes for: performances, commissions, recordings, etc.). Nurturing those relationships has resulted in the most beautiful friendships of my life, as well as some really wonderful professional opportunities.

To build your network, first identify which factors you can and cannot control. You can't control who likes, programs, and commissions your music. But you do have control over many aspects of this career:

- How and when you reach out to new contacts who could hire you in the future
- How and when you bring up money in conversations with your peers
- How you position yourself and your work within your community in a way that facilitates future collaborations

Chapter 1 asked how you are serving your community with the music you create. That question is especially important at the start of your career, but it never ceases to be relevant. Some composers make an entire career out of building a musical community, through starting an ensemble or cultivating a fan base and then serving that community.

Juhi Bansal notes that to find your community, "you need to go meet musicians. You need to go to concerts. You need to build those relationships." Jocelyn Hagen believes in a similar approach. "I do believe in the power of networking," she says, "and you have to be willing and ready to start a

Composing a Living. Brandon Elliott and Dale Trumbore, Oxford University Press.
© Brandon Elliott and Dale Trumbore 2025. DOI: 10.1093/9780197803509.003.0003

conversation and to pitch [your] ideas." For Hagen, it's very important to find the right people—collaborators whose values align with your own.

In order to build community, what good are you willing to do for others? You may find it helpful to return to the following questions throughout your career:

- Are you occasionally passing along your peers' best work to conductors with whom you've collaborated?
- Are you attending your peers' concerts and events?
- Are you sharing your colleagues' new recordings with your friends?
- When you turn down a job, are you then referring colleagues who might be a better fit for that gig?

Doing the above without any expectation of return requires trust that goodwill will eventually come back to you. You may also experience personal satisfaction from seeing others succeed, knowing that you played a small role in their success. This feeling is a missing piece in many musicians' careers. While you may be satisfied with your musical progress and accomplishments, you may not find the professional *and* personal fulfillment you seek unless you are also helping others.

Working with Friends

Community Building

Aside from collaborative relationships, you can grow your composing community by seeking out like-minded composers who inspire you to grow your own craft. "Are the people that you're running with creating music that you also find valuable or interesting?" asks Zanaida Stewart Robles. "That's your club." Robles feels her work is better when she's spending time with peers whose music she values.

Isaac Io Schankler recommends that composition students seek out people who are close in age to them, at a similar stage in their career path, or a little bit ahead of them, particularly in fields like multimedia composition or composing for electronics. "Everything changes so fast with music and the arts and money," Schankler says. "The income streams have in some ways changed really radically." While professors may be able to give you standard advice on joining a performing rights organization (PRO) and collecting royalties from various income streams, their knowledge on your specific niche of composing—and the most up-to-date ways to form a business around that niche—may be out of date. As a composer who has written music for independent video games and electro-acoustic ensembles, Schankler wishes they had sought out more advice from their peers earlier in their career.

Composing for Friends

Writing music for friends is an effective way to strengthen your musical community while also honing your craft. Seek out collaborations with artists you respect as human beings *and* creators. These individuals might be musicians, or their talents could extend to other artistic fields, as discussed in Chapter 1; you might initiate collaborations with choreographers, directors, writers, photographers, or other artists. Many early-career composers start working with fellow creators in college, then realize after graduation that these collaborative relationships can persist and grow throughout an entire career.

In general, the more composing experience you have, the better. Dale Trumbore believes firmly in iterating throughout your work: always seeking a better version of the techniques you've used and the choices you've made in the past. She calls this "fixing it forward," putting any mistakes or changes you wish you had made into future pieces rather than constantly revising older work. One way to rapidly "fix it forward" is to compose for as many collaborators as possible, always aiming to write a better piece than your last—or at least to never make the same mistake twice.

Many composers gain this early experience through writing for their friends. You may also find that your friend-collaborators are often willing to perform whatever you write for them. Even if these collaborations pay little to no money in commission fees, you'll still receive tremendous value from the experience, gaining deeper insight into each friend's performance preferences. Additionally, your friends may also offer more thoughtful or truthful feedback than other collaborators. In a partnership where you and your collaborator feel comfortable offering suggestions and gently proposing revisions as needed, you may feel comfortable writing more audacious music, exploring the extreme outer ranges of a voice or instrument, or venturing into new (or new to you) extended techniques. You can find all of these experiences in a paid collaboration as well as an unpaid or bartered one, but as an early-career composer, the payoff from even low-paying or unpaid projects can add priceless value to your growth as an artist.

Composer Collectives

Some composers find value in starting a collective: a group of two or more composers who work together, like Bang on a Can, the new-music ensemble founded by Michael Gordon, David Lang, and Julia Wolfe. Sharing resources through a collective allows composers to uplift their work simultaneously while splitting the costs of more expensive musical endeavors. This sharing of resources could include presenting concerts, recording albums, presenting or exhibiting at a conference, composing collaboratively, reaching out to conductors, or hiring a publicist or assistant as a group rather than as individuals.

However, you don't need to form a collective in order to pursue the activities mentioned here, like putting on a concert or recording an album with your peers. These collaborative efforts may make the most sense if you write similar music—or compose within a similar genre—to that of your collaborators. There are also upsides to having close composer friends who write in different genres, though. For example, if you compose primarily for wind ensemble and your best composer friend writes choral music, you may feel more comfortable asking each other questions about the money and business side of composition, knowing that you are not in direct competition.

Friendly Competition

It is a standard business practice to adjust prices based on the prices of your competitors. Composers may be hesitant to share their rates if they view their peers as rivals, and from a purely business standpoint, you *are* in direct competition with your peers. But in many composer relationships, friendships prevail over that competitive spirit. Even if you are theoretically "in competition" with a peer—you both compose for the same types of ensembles—that doesn't mean you can't still have a wonderful, collaborative friendship.

For Brandon Elliott, the ultimate goal of a business relationship is this: the relationship you have with a collaborator is so meaningful that even when you are not in the room, your collaborator wants to bring your name into the conversation whenever an opportunity arises. That only happens with a strong relationship that's built over time, and it's not something you can force. For instance, a composer wouldn't say to a conductor, "I know we're friends, so I'd really appreciate it if you would name drop me for future opportunities!" But the mark of a sincere collaborative friendship is that you mutually want to help each other. You want to see your collaborator succeed, and they want the same for you.

Composer friendships have been crucial to the success of Dale Trumbore's career. With close composer friends, she feels comfortable speaking openly and honestly about commissioning rates and score pricing. Several friends have shared templates for commissions or royalties with Trumbore, and she is happy to share hers in turn. Beyond the more technical aspects of composition, close composer friendships allow for frank discussions about the unique difficulties of a composing career, including burnout, anxiety, and navigating problematic collaborations.

At least two of Trumbore's commissions were a direct result of a close friend's referral, and she regularly recommends talented friends' work to conductors looking to expand their programming. The firsthand endorsement of a colleague or peer is far more powerful than any social media post, marketing, or self-promotion. Having a strong social media presence or hiring a publicist can absolutely help your career, and these options certainly don't hurt your prospects or your opportunities. Still, these factors are no substitute for relationship building.

The Value of Relationships

Early collaborations with friends often take shape through barter or other non-monetary exchanges. More than one composer we spoke to joked about the "writing a piece of music in exchange for a piece of pizza" commissioning model. While Abbie Betinis encourages young composers not to compose for free, she recognizes value in non-monetary forms of currency. Early in Betinis's career, she was happy to write a piece in exchange for a great recording or for inclusion on a tour with multiple performances. You may find that in your own career, the non-monetary value of your music reaching new audiences on an international tour or through a professional album recording is also worth accepting a smaller (or even nonexistent) commissioning fee. If your music is being performed multiple times, your performing rights royalties from those performances can also help balance out what a more traditional commission would have paid.

You may find it helpful to assign a monetary value to these intangibles as you weigh variables beyond money. As an example, let's say you would really like to produce an album of your chamber music, but it would cost $10,000 to record. Let's also assume your commissioning fee is $1,000 per minute of completed music when you are writing a new commission for chamber ensemble. In this example, a string quartet approaches you to write a new ten-minute piece, and they're offering you $2,500—a rate that you might usually view as too low. Normally, you would quote your fee as $10,000 (10 minutes × $1,000 per minute). However, this quartet also wants to commercially record an album featuring the new commission alongside your two previous works for string quartet. If you have decided an album of your chamber music is worth $10,000, then the total value of this commission becomes $12,500 ($2,500 commissioning fee + $10,000 in perceived value).

You could use the same approach of assigning value to non-monetary factors when bartering for your music. While bartering relationships are less common in composition, some composers trade their skills—composing or otherwise—for career benefits. For example, you might write a new composition for a friend who can't afford to pay you money, but in exchange they help with your website design. Or you might barter your own skills, teaching a colleague composition lessons in exchange for their editing, mixing, and mastering your album of solo piano music. Betinis's above examples—writing new pieces in exchange for well-produced recordings or inclusion on a multi-performance tour—illustrate other successful approaches to bartering.

While a bartering exchange doesn't have to be an exact trade in value, you may still find it helpful to carry out the exercise above: assign approximate monetary value to appraise a non-monetary exchange. Perhaps you would like to study Spanish, and a singer friend fluent in that language wants you to write them a new song cycle. They could trade you twenty hours of Spanish tutoring valued at $150 per hour in exchange for an art song commission valued at $3,000. Or if you are trading composition lessons for a colleague's hours spent engineering your album, you might value your teaching hours at the same price as your colleague's hourly engineering rate. Rates can vary drastically, and the better you know your collaborator, the more flexible your bartering arrangement may be. Regardless, consider creating a letter of agreement for a bartering arrangement to solidify your mutually-agreed-upon terms. (Chapter 10 will discuss contract terms in greater detail.)

Nurturing Long-Term Relationships

As you cultivate early-career collaborations, you are also laying the groundwork for future opportunities, should your collaborators eventually find higher-profile work. Maybe one or more of your peers will accept an academic job with the budget to bring you in for a week-long teaching residency. Maybe a performer friend will accept a steady gig with a professional orchestra and eventually commission a concerto from you. Maybe another friend whose student films you scored in college will hire you for their first feature film.

Derrick Skye's relationships with conductors have been particularly important for securing performances and commissions. "You have got to get to know and be friends with the conductors," he says, "because they'll take you to the moon. If they really love what you're doing, they're going to take you with them." Similarly, Abbie Betinis finds tremendous value in the people—conductors, performers, and other fans—who get as excited as she does about her music. "They are my best megaphone," she says. "They're my best connector." Rather than pay for a publicist, Betinis invests in her relationships with these "megaphone people" who essentially serve as one-person marketing teams advocating for Betinis's compositions.

As your network grows, you may find it helpful to rely on tools to help you maintain and cultivate relationships. This can be particularly useful as people begin to program your music without first forming the kind of personal relationship described by Skye and Betinis. Customer Relationship Management (CRM) software programs keep track of everyone you know, logging every interaction—like score sales, commissions, emails, and texts—that you have with collaborators and potential future customers. While it may feel strange to track your closest collaborator-friends in a software program, this system is particularly effective for keeping track of collaborators you may have only met once. (For a list of current CRM software options, see the Resources section.)

Fostering Relationships with Fans

For Eric Whitacre, building a relationship with a fan base—including getting to know people after concerts—is just as important as building relationships with performers. He models his approach after some pop and rock bands, who "need a relatively small, passionate fan base." Whitacre notes that you don't actually need millions of fans to have a career in this field. "After every performance I'll stay and I'll meet as many people as want to meet me," he says. When you make the effort to talk to fans, "you're connecting in a very genuine way with the people who are interested in what you're doing, and you get to meet so many incredible people."

Whitacre realized early on—when he wrote his piece *Water Night* at age twenty-four—that emotional connection was crucial to his career. He composed *Water Night* on a sixty-one-key synthesizer, playing with "goopy analog sounds to emulate what a choir was going to sound like," he says. Even using a synthesizer, he could tell that he'd written something he found profoundly beautiful—something true.

> When you're a composer and you have that feeling, try to have confidence that that feeling will then be felt by other people. That's the thing that's going to make the career. Not the name that's attached to it, not the publishing, not the marketing of it. . . . How many times did anyone ever perform a piece because it was on the front page of the Hal Leonard catalog, or the Schirmer catalog? Actually what happens [more often] is some other conductor says, "You've got to perform this. You're not going to believe how great this is." Or even better, a student comes to them and says, "I heard this online. We have to do this this year." The single most important factor is the emotional connection.

Encouraging Future Collaborations

How should you nurture relationships with future collaborators? Consider keeping "gently in touch." If you don't know a collaborator well, you don't want to spam them with multiple requests to look at your music. Instead, you may want to approach that relationship as you would a friendship, trying to get to know that person on a human level first. If you are hoping to speak with a potential collaborator who doesn't live in your city, you could suggest a brief video chat: a "virtual coffee" rather than an in-person one. And if you are reaching out for advice to someone you don't know very well, you are much more likely to receive an answer to one very specific question than you are to a five-paragraph-long message.

Querying with a Single, Specific Question

This technique works especially well when you are reaching out to a more established professional, who may dread responding to open-ended, ambiguous questions as well as ones they've already answered elsewhere. In other words, a question like "How did you decide which publisher was right for you?" is much easier and quicker to answer than a question like "How did you get started in music, and what are five steps I could take toward becoming as successful as you?" The latter question has likely already been answered in interviews or articles about that collaborator. Note that starting a conversation with a single question could later result in an extended dialogue with your contact, leaving room for a more expansive conversation or even mentorship in the future.

Writing a Cold Email

The above approach is also true of cold emails: the shorter and more efficient, the better. In keeping a message brief, you demonstrate respect for your potential collaborator's time and limited resources. When you first reach out to a new contact, consider the 1-2-3 method:

- Include **one** sentence introducing yourself.
- Write potential future collaborators a brief message of up to **two** paragraphs.
- Send no more than **three** examples of your work as links, not attachments.

Think of how you react when you receive an email from someone you don't know: You may approach that email with a certain degree of wariness. When you send a cold email, it will likely be better received if you can find a connection to "warm" it up. In messages, as with a real-life introduction, it can be helpful to have a mutual acquaintance introduce you rather than reaching out cold. If a mutual friend introduces you, your prospective collaborator will perceive you first as a friend-of-a-friend rather than as a stranger asking for a favor.

If you're reaching out to a soloist, ensemble, or conductor *without* an acquaintance in common, you can "warm up" your message in other ways. Your email could mention something you have in common. Perhaps you and the recipient of your message both attended the same university, for example, or you hail from the same state, currently reside in the same city, or studied with the same teacher. Your email could also offer specific praise for one of your prospective collaborator's past performances or recordings; perhaps they recorded your favorite interpretation of a piece, or you attended and loved their latest concert.

If you are cold-contacting someone about them potentially performing your music, research their programming preferences before you pass along your work samples. Are you familiar with the kind of repertoire they traditionally program? Does your music logically fit into that programming, or is it drastically different from what they usually perform? Do you have compositions that not only fit the instrumentation of their ensemble, but also have similar thematic or other elements in common with music they've performed in the past? Send two or three links to samples of your work that not only showcase your skills, but also fit the programming needs of the conductor, soloist, or ensemble you are contacting. This extra step proves to your recipient that you have taken the time to consider their unique preferences. As a result, your music is more likely to be considered for performance.

Attending Conferences

In-person conferences offer a meaningful chance to connect in person with those you may only know through a screen or through social media. Many music communities offer larger, national conferences—like the American Choral Directors Association National Conference and the Midwest Clinic International Band and Orchestra Festival—as well as smaller, more regional conferences.

Isaac Io Schankler points out that those smaller conferences may be a better starting place for composers hoping to network. In Schankler's experience as a video game composer, the Game Developers Conference (GDC) can be helpful for mid- to late-career composers, but perhaps intimidating for composers at the start of a career. "I would say sometimes the big conferences like GDC are, counterintuitively, maybe less useful if you're just starting out, because it's like this huge melting pot of people, and everyone's looking for work right now," Schankler says. "But smaller conferences that are maybe more niche or more local are great ways to meet people and to be part of a community."

Schankler's conference advice extends beyond video games into any discipline. If you are near the start of your career, you may want to prioritize attending statewide or regional conferences over national ones. As you attend conferences, consider that you are playing a long game. In Dale Trumbore's experience, it takes an average of two years to transition from meeting a conductor for the first time to working with them on a performance or commission. If you view your networking efforts from this perspective, you can relax: your goal upon meeting a new potential collaborator is simply to make a good impression, not to push them toward an immediate collaboration. Use the principles provided in this book to stay in touch over those two years.

Showcasing Your Work

When you are seeking future collaborations, it's important to have demonstrable proof of concept: evidence that you are pleasant to work with and you create excellent work. If a past collaborator wants to recommend you to their colleague, what elements can they reference to show that you compose excellent music?

For many composers, these elements are high-quality recordings and perusal scores that can easily be viewed online. This particular intersection of relationship building and proof of concept—the need for high-quality examples of your music—has led composer Derrick Skye to prioritize both creating full-length albums of his work and pricing score sales affordably. Skye releases these recordings not necessarily to get a million people to stream his tracks, he says, but so that any potential collaborators considering his music can find his music on a streaming service and listen to it instantly. A website is another way to showcase your work, allowing future collaborators to easily search for you and find your music and biography.

Test-Driving Collaborations

You may find it valuable to track who is commissioning you and how they discovered your work. Reena Esmail, a self-proclaimed fan of Excel, created a spreadsheet to track her commissions, see where they originated, and trace the degrees of separation between her and her commissioners. In doing so, she discovered that her earliest commissions came from performers and conductors she knew personally or those separated by one degree from her immediate connections. Many of those collaborations continued to grow over time. As Esmail's career progressed, her commissions originated from sources several degrees away from her initial network. The people Esmail worked with in the past were recommending her work to their friends and colleagues, who in turn were recommending her work to *their* friends and colleagues. Others were discovering her music organically through concerts, festivals, and conferences.

Now, as an established composer, Esmail finds that her commissions often come from strangers. As her music has taken on a life of its own, she is so many degrees separated from those commission requests that she can no longer trace them back to one person recommending or advocating for her music. For Esmail, writing each new commission feels incredibly personal: "I'm giving whoever I'm working with a piece of my soul, right? That's what you're doing when you're a composer, and it's not a transactional thing." Especially when you are mining your most personal experiences for your work, you'll want to ensure that you are working with collaborators who will respect your time, your art, and your boundaries.

Esmail suggests that composers work with potential future commissioners on an existing piece of their music before collaborating on a new project. This way, when you do embark on a commission with that performer or ensemble, you'll already have the foundations of a relationship in place, along with valuable information about how they approach collaboration. Do they prepare your work with respect and care? Just as important, do they treat *you* with respect and care? Is collaborating with them a meaningful experience, or does it feel detached and impersonal? After your "trial run" of collaboration on an existing piece, you'll know whether that working relationship feels like a good fit before committing to a months- or even years-long commission.

This advice and the following section on red flags may be most relevant to mid-career and established composers, who may have a larger portfolio of existing compositions and may be in a more flexible position to turn down paid work than early-career composers.

Avoiding Red Flags

Alex Shapiro notes that there may be moments when your gut instinct tells you *not* to work with a certain collaborator. "You've probably been there in your life—I have in mine—when you know it doesn't feel right. For whatever reason, there's just something creepy about the clients, and it's not feeling good early on," she says. Shapiro has vowed to avoid that feeling—and those potential clients—as much as possible, and has found herself happier in her work as a result. Of course, she notes, this is easier to do when you've reached the point in your career when you can pick and choose your projects. But even if you are not in a position to turn down work, "listen to your gut," Shapiro urges. "The overriding thing is to trust your gut instinct, and when you feel a red flag or a cringe moment—as I like to call it, when your 'cringeometer' starts to ping—pay attention to that."

These red flags could range from a very specific, identifiable "off" factor, like a collaborator blatantly disrespecting you, to a vague feeling that something is wrong. When you first begin your composing career, you may be more inclined to say yes to nearly any paid job writing music, but especially as your career progresses, learning to say "no" becomes just as important as saying "yes" (a topic discussed in more depth at the end of Chapter 6). But as you learn to identify what feels amiss about certain projects—and carefully observe how those collaborations play out if you do ignore your gut instincts—you'll be better prepared to avoid similarly "cringey" projects in the future. It's never too early in your career to decline a project if you're dreading having to work with a potential collaborator.

Let's say you have learned to trust your instincts in collaborations, are growing your network of creative collaborators, and are beginning to build your sustainable music career. What's next? In the following chapter, you'll learn how to handle the stresses that pop up when you pursue a career in composition. For many composers, these mental demons arrive in the form of voices insisting that you don't deserve to make a living writing music, that no one will pay you for your compositions, or that everyone you know is more talented and successful than you. In learning to dismantle that negative mindset in favor of a more successful one, you'll cultivate a sense of self-worth as you gain experience throughout your career.

3

Cultivating a Successful Mindset

Carving out a career in music can be intimidating, frustrating, and downright scary. In the interviews for this book, most composers shared common fears or had held those fears at the start of their careers. Some of these fears are related to talent and creative success; others relate to money, business, and legal practices. You may have experienced some of the same concerns:

- The fear that you are not talented enough to "make it" as a composer.
- The fear that you'll never make enough money to support yourself with your music.
- The fear that when it comes to money, business, and legal matters, you are not smart enough to learn the principles necessary to succeed.
- The fear that you are not worthy of success.
- The fear that your colleagues are better than you.
- The fear that if you work a "day job," particularly a non-musical one, you aren't as worthy or successful as a full-time composer.
- The fear that you'll never have enough saved for retirement.
- The fear that if you quote a high rate, a collaborator will choose someone else.
- The fear that if you turn down a job, no more work will come.
- The fear that this career is filled with nothing but rejection.

This book will dismantle these internal fears, one by one, and later chapters will teach you strategies to manage the necessary financial and legal aspects of your business. Much of the negative thinking that you'll have to overcome, though, is rooted in societal perspectives toward music, and you'll be best served by learning to work through these negative viewpoints early on in your career. The most insidious of these is the phrase mentioned in the Introduction: *No one makes a living writing music.*

When Juhi Bansal embarked on a career as a musician, she didn't think it was possible to make a living as a professional composer, and that is one reason why she had "a long detour into teaching before coming back to freelancing," she says. "Obviously it is possible [to make a living in music], particularly with

Composing a Living. Brandon Elliott and Dale Trumbore, Oxford University Press.
© Brandon Elliott and Dale Trumbore 2025. DOI: 10.1093/9780197803509.003.0004

technology and the way it's made self-publishing and distribution and marketing much easier than they used to be."

The composers featured here demonstrate that not only can you make a living in music, but you can even thrive while doing so. Perhaps a more helpful, accurate phrase than *No one makes a living writing music* is this: *There's no single right way to make a living writing music.* The most successful musicians combine passive and active composing income to support themselves and their families. Many find a balance of two or more jobs that fulfill them, which may or may not include teaching and performing alongside composing. These side jobs may not involve music at all.

In the field of composition, there's no corporate ladder to ascend, no guaranteed annual salary or bonus, and no set combination of college degrees that will assure you a steady job. It can be much harder to forge a career in this field than others. But plenty of people *do* make a living writing music; that fact is indisputable. If you want to be one of them, be prepared for years of working on your craft, thinking strategically about your business practices, and carefully calibrating your income streams. (Chapter 7 will address passive and active income stream options for composers.) Above all, be ready to adapt and grow as you face new challenges with every step of this career.

Evolving Careers, Evolving Challenges

Growing your career isn't necessarily enough to mitigate the common fears mentioned at the start of this chapter. Rather, as you gain experience in your career, you may find yourself facing new and different obstacles, along with new and different concerns. For many composers, each new level of success brings a new set of worries. Sometimes even a single performance or one high-paying commission is enough to launch an avalanche of confusion or frustration. Working through a new challenge may not be a pleasant experience, but each one offers an opportunity to overcome your fears and implement a lasting solution. For example, consider the following scenarios:

Scenario 1

New success: A less-experienced composer's piece is programmed at a prominent international festival. The composer has self-published this work. After the performance, many conductors want to commission the composer and buy their scores. The composer also receives an offer from a publisher to publish that composition.

Questions and challenges:

- Should they consider placing their work with the traditional publisher, work with a music distributor, or continue to self-publish?
- The composer isn't sure whether they're charging appropriate rates for score sales or commissions.

Common reactions and fears:

- "This is overwhelming—I'll never be smart enough to make good business decisions."
- "My music isn't worth the high rates that other composers are charging."
- "Am I making the right decisions? How would I know if I am?"

Possible solutions:

- The composer researches what peers are charging for score sales, and they price their work within that range.
- They ask several trusted peers and mentors the following questions: "What do you think I should be charging for a commission of this scope?" and "What has your experience been like navigating traditional publishing, distribution, and self-publishing options?" After weighing the pros and cons of these options, they make an informed choice.

Scenario 2

New Success: A composer's film-scoring career is going well this year, and they've just received the final payment for their biggest project to date. They're on track to make 200 percent more annual income than they made the previous year.

Questions and challenges:

- When a composer is ready to incorporate as a business entity, where do they start? Whom do they approach?
- Because the composer is earning more money this year, they need to set aside more money to pay quarterly estimated taxes.
- They are aware they could form a tax-advantaged corporation or LLC, but that idea is daunting.

Common reactions and fears:

- "Establishing a corporation is way too complicated—I'll never be able to understand that process, so I shouldn't bother."
- "Maybe I should have made less money, because then I'd owe less on my taxes."

Possible solutions:

- The composer schedules a free initial meeting with an accountant to discuss how much money they should be contributing toward their estimated quarterly taxes.
- They also ask the accountant whether it makes sense to incorporate now, and which entity would make sense for their income level. With the accountant's help, they understand the tax advantages of incorporating.

Scenario 3

New success: A composer is approached for three new commissions, but the anticipated deadlines for these projects fall within two weeks of each other. One project doesn't pay much but is a collaboration with a respected colleague. One pays generously, but the composer finds the project uninspiring. One pays fairly well, and the composer is confident that the piece could be written quickly.

Questions and challenges:

- How can they balance these three projects, completing each one on time, with a feeling of ease rather than panic? The composer doesn't know whether it's possible to fit these new commissions into such a tight schedule.
- How do they weigh the merits and downsides of each of these projects?
- Which commission(s), if any, should they turn down?

Common reactions and fears:

- "I can't raise my rates or commissioners will stop hiring me."
- "If I turn down a commission, that ensemble will never want to program my music again."
- "Even though these three deadlines are basically impossible to meet on time, I need to take on all of these projects. I can't afford to turn down work."

Possible solutions:

- The composer realistically assesses their monthly expenses and the time needed to complete each piece.
- With this information, the composer creates a timeline with internal deadlines that allows them to accept the collaboration with their respected colleague and the fast, fairly well-paying project.
- The composer reaches out to the commissioner for the uninspiring but generously paid project to suggest a more engaging version of the project (e.g., a different text, a change of theme, or the addition of a soloist) and inquire about writing the work for the following season or another future concert. If the commissioner says no, the composer accepts that the project wasn't the right fit at this time.
- The next time they are offered a commission, they quote a higher rate.

A career in music can feel like a game of Whac-A-Mole. When you solve one problem, like finally making enough composing income to cover your rent, you'll often find another problem has replaced it, like needing to set aside more money to cover higher taxes. This has certainly been true in Trumbore's career, and she has turned to colleague-friends and tax professionals to ask nearly all of the theoretical "questions and challenges" mentioned above: "Am I charging enough for my commissions?" "Is it time for me to incorporate as a business?" "What's the right way to turn down a commission?"

As shown above, there's a possible solution to each new obstacle. As your career grows, so too can your capacity to handle challenges. Don't let these daunting concerns derail you; the later chapters of this book will address many of the specific business, money, and tax-related concerns listed in the above scenarios.

Cultivating a healthy mindset around your art and business—embracing thoughts like "The work I create has inherent value" and "I can learn what I don't know"—can be crucial to your success in this uncertain and ever-evolving career field. A positive mindset alone will not be enough to guarantee success in your career. But you can cultivate an inherent sense that you are already worthy and complete apart from your music, and no success or failure can take that from you.

Cultivating Self-Worth and Healthy Relationships

Timothy C. Takach notes that every musician starts their career with questions of "How much do I charge?" and "How much am I worth?" He wishes he'd known when he started that "the relationship between yourself, your collaborators and your income is this flexible and negotiable thing. . . . There is no one correct answer that you could give somebody." As a creator, you get to decide what your value is. When you are new to composing, many variables will justify lowering that value, Takach says: "You're just getting started. You've not done this before. You're still learning. You're not well known yet." These factors can chip away at your sense of self-worth and lead you to negotiate a number down in your mind even before you speak a rate out loud to a potential collaborator.

But Takach has noticed that he can employ the opposite approach, telling himself, "Let's up [this rate] and see what happens." Often, he finds that the collaborator will accept the requested rate. "That's an extra [however many] dollars in my wallet because I had the confidence to ask for it." With projects he's less enthusiastic to say yes to, he'll quote an even higher rate. If a collaborator says no, he's fine letting the project go; if they say yes, he's getting paid very well for his time. If Takach is approached about a project he really wants to accept, he'll ask for what he wants to be paid, then say, "I really want to make this happen, so let me know what budget you're working with, and we can certainly talk from there." This accomplishes two goals: it lets a collaborator know the fee you are hoping to get, and it lets them know that you have some flexibility.

To cultivate a sense of self-worth, some artists keep a "brag file"—a digital or physical record of their career successes, compliments on their work, and overall achievements. When they're feeling down about a recent failure, this file reminds them of the milestones they've already achieved. The success of this approach lies not only in how it may remind you of your accomplishments, but in how it emphasizes a long-term career trajectory. Keeping a "brag file" for years or even decades offers a big-picture view that can put any single failure into a much broader perspective.

You may experience moments where you look at your composer peers and feel that they're all more successful than you: they're making more money than you, they're being offered higher-profile jobs, or their music is being programmed by better-known ensembles. It's common to feel discouraged by others' achievements, as if their success comes at your expense.

The success of your close peers, however, can actually be a great thing. If you cultivate friendships with colleagues who are at your level or even more experienced in this field, they can become trusted resources. You can turn to them for advice on setting your rates, finding a good accountant or assistant, and navigating other obstacles in this field. When these successful colleagues have to decline a job or otherwise find themselves in the position to refer work, you may be first on their list of referrals. In many ways, it's in your best interest to foster relationships with people who are thriving in their music careers. The more you cultivate genuine friendships with your peers, the more you'll feel pride in their accomplishments instead of jealousy or self-disparagement.

For better or worse, various elements will calibrate the ease or difficulty of every composer's career. Weigh your achievements and those of your peers with these advantages in mind, then return your focus to your own resources and the factors you can control. Continue developing and expanding your network of smart, talented, like-minded collaborators. When you love collaborating with someone, your relationship with that collaborator—and their steadfast belief in you—can be enough to sustain you through a moment of self-doubt. Take advantage of the resources you have at hand, and when you find yourself in a place to share those resources, ask again how you can contribute to your community.

Working through Negative Feedback

Just as praise from a collaborator can bolster your confidence, harsh criticism from a mentor or respected colleague can be enough to derail your sense of self-worth. Overcoming negative feedback of any kind can be a challenge, and that feedback can arrive in the form of direct criticism, a bad review, or something heard secondhand.

Zanaida Stewart Robles is no stranger to working through negative feedback. When someone tells you your work isn't good enough, she says, "It can shut you down, and it did shut me down, and now I wish it hadn't." Robles wishes she'd had a support system or collective of composer colleagues to help her reject or process the early harsh feedback she received. But because she didn't have that support system, she allowed the feedback to deter her. As a result of those negative experiences, she says, "I think I lost probably ten years on a composing career."

What was even more damaging than that criticism, though, was the way Robles felt when people she respected rejected her work. "That's the thing that I continue to struggle with: How [could] this person I went to for support react in a way that made me feel so bad?"

Now, as an established composer, performer, and educator, Robles has not only cultivated more resiliency but also has the opportunity to instill inner self-confidence in her students. Robles encourages her students to shake off negative feedback. She reinforces their reasons for composing, asking, "Do you love to do this? Do you want to continue doing this? And do you believe in this piece? What do you like about it? If you believe in the piece, and you love this process, then how could you have been rejected?" After that reframing, Robles has found that her students can usually see whether there's a kernel of truth in the negative feedback—actionable advice they can apply to a revision or to future work—or whether that feedback was, as Robles puts it, "trash."

Dara Taylor has similarly useful strategies that allow her to accept and incorporate negative feedback into her film scores. One such strategy is recognizing that film scoring is a "team sport." "I love getting good notes that make things better," she says, especially when feedback about her music encourages her to reconsider the point of view in a scene or let a moment remain silent. She observes that it's much easier to take feedback from trusted colleagues. "When you work with people that you like, it's a lot easier to take notes from them," she says. "They're not saying you are bad; they're not saying this music is bad. They're just saying that this may not work for this moment, and maybe there's a moment later on in this film that this works for, or maybe it lives in your graveyard and you can use it for something else." Deciding not to be precious about her music has made Taylor's film scoring process much easier.

Negative feedback is an unpleasant reality of a composing career, and you may find it helpful to employ certain mindset shifts as you encounter criticism. Remember that all feedback is subjective. Since there is no single correct way to craft a melody, set a word to music, or structure a piece, your solution for how to solve a problem may be drastically different from another composer's opinion.

If your music is rejected by a competition, grant application, or publisher, remind yourself that there may be nothing wrong with the music. As Dara Taylor explains above, that music is simply not the right fit for this opportunity, which is not the same as being objectively "bad." When you are rejected from an opportunity to which hundreds of musicians have applied, that system guarantees failure for all but a handful of applicants. That failure is a feature of the system, not a moral failing on your part.

Valuing Your Time

The music you create is inherently valuable because your life is valuable. In creating music, you are choosing to dedicate your precious hours to creating art. It's never too early in your career to start thinking this way: *Your time is valuable.*

While the word "currency" almost always refers to money, consider it here as a valuable factor that can be traded for other valuable factors. Your time is valuable because you can trade it for money, yes, but you can also spend your time building relationships and investing in yourself. Ultimately, time is the most valuable currency you have in your career and your life. Brandon Elliott often tells his music students that when they say "no" to an opportunity, they're saying "yes" to themselves and to their time. When you decline an opportunity, take the time you saved and put it to good use.

When Sydney Guillaume first walked away from a commission that wouldn't meet his minimum fee, he wondered if he'd made the right decision. It's common for composers to feel this way about turning down opportunities, especially when they rely on commissioning fees for half or more of their overall income. Now, when Guillaume walks away from an opportunity, he tells himself that he's keeping that space open for another one to show up. "There have been times where I've actually had to turn down a commission" because of a full schedule, he says. As a result, he no longer wants to accept low-paying or uninspiring commissions, because they could prevent him from taking on more fulfilling, higher-paying work. In this way, Guillaume's mindset around self-worth and the value of his time continues to evolve as his career unfolds.

Defining Success

Re-evaluating your own definition of success can also help you cultivate a sense of worth. As you establish your composing career and build a strong sense of self, consider questions like the following:

- What drives you?
- What motivates your music?
- What values do you express in your music?
- What qualities do you look for in your ideal collaborators?
- Who are you when you are *not* writing music?

Thomas Kotcheff acknowledges that part of being a composer is doing what you do well, but also "not being afraid to do something different, then abandon ship if it didn't go right." Kotcheff taught composition at a university for a year—what he'd thought would be the logical next stage of his career after getting his doctorate—but soon realized he hated teaching at a collegiate level. "The path is so unexplainable sometimes," he says. Rather than following any prescribed journey, he suggests composers should move forward, try new things, and say yes as often as possible, but "stop when it's not right." No composing job is more important than your mental and physical well-being.

Composers who don't take time off or cultivate passions outside their work are at a greater risk for burning out. These composers may also feel a sense of dread and fatigue around their work rather than an electrifying will to create. As you shape your definition of success, consider factors within and outside of your career—factors that include your mental and physical health. What kind of life are you building? Many composers have monetary ambitions for their careers: a certain amount they'd like to earn per year, or a target number for score sales and other royalties. But as you consider your financial goals, a healthier approach may be to ask yourself what kind of life you are hoping to build with that money and what elements of that life you already have. Are you spending your time in ways that align with your goals and your ideal life? (This book's Conclusion will address the varied way that composers answer this question, offering several different perspectives on what it means to be a successful composer.)

No "Right Answers"

As you strive for your definition of success, the balance between your work and other parts of your life—family, friends, free time, and hobbies among them—will evolve in an ongoing equation. You don't need to have the "right answers" for how to balance your time; you'll learn by doing, and your body will let you know if you are overworking. Listen to those signals. Above all, maintaining a flexible and positive mindset around your composing career means controlling what you can and, as Derrick Skye suggests, learning to love what you don't know. "I could say it a thousand times: just be confident," he says. "Be comfortable with what you don't know, and be comfortable with your will to find out. And then you're going to be all right."

4

Goals and Economics

A Strategic Balance

Many composers have grand visions for a career, but big dreams can be overwhelming if you try to tackle them all at once. You may look at other musicians further ahead in their careers and desire what they have: high-paying, high-profile work with famous collaborators, or royalties that provide them enough passive income to never have to work again. You may be tempted to set your goals similarly high, aiming for stratospheric royalty statements and collaborations with top ensembles. The biggest challenge in goal setting, though, is transforming your dreams into achievable actions. Navigating the goal-setting process is crucial for long-term success, and this chapter will help you break down ambitious plans into manageable steps and sustainable systems. You will also learn how to weigh the economic advantages and disadvantages of each project. This chapter may even encourage you to change the way you set goals altogether, prioritizing meaningful work and systems over outcomes.

Create Systems to Reach Your Goals

When contemplating an ambitious goal, your instinct may be to create a frustratingly long to-do list. While to-do lists are helpful for organizing daily or weekly tasks, big goals are often better served by a different framework. Instead of starting with a list of tasks, consider zooming out to identify the systems necessary to bring about your particular objective. These systems might include regular practice routines, continuous learning, and networking. They provide a framework to support your career growth and guide your overall direction regardless of specific outcomes, and this subtle difference is important for sustainable success.

Let's use strength training as an example. Your goal might be to gain a certain amount of lean muscle mass or easily lift a certain weight. The systems

Composing a Living. Brandon Elliott and Dale Trumbore, Oxford University Press.
© Brandon Elliott and Dale Trumbore 2025. DOI: 10.1093/9780197803509.003.0005

necessary to make that aspiration a reality involve spending an increasing amount of time under tension and creating a means to measure your progress (e.g., performing a certain number of repetitions or increasing the weight lifted). As you follow your systems, your goal will become much more inherent, attainable, and sustainable. You are likely to reach your goal by following these routines, but even if you fail to meet whatever arbitrary numbers you've set as a goal, you'll still find yourself in stronger shape as a result of following the systems.

Similarly, if your goal is to compose your first symphony, you may need to start by identifying the end goal and then work backward, outlining each step required to achieve it. What will you need in place to have your symphony performed? You'll need a conductor and an orchestra willing to perform the piece. You'll need to have composed a significant amount of music, likely in multiple movements. You'll need substantial knowledge about how to write music for orchestra, including familiarity with the ranges and technical capabilities of each instrument.

If you were to use a systems-based approach to write a large orchestral work without a commission, you might break down that goal into the following practices.

- Cultivate relationships with conductors, performers, and other administrative individuals who work with orchestras. Allow yourself a reasonable period of time to form connections (e.g., two years).
- Nurture any existing relationships with orchestral performers, who can give you feedback on individual orchestral parts.
- Score-study symphonies and other orchestral works, analyzing different techniques and approaches to orchestration.
- Establish a composing practice (e.g., compose for at least an hour a day, four days a week).
- Consider writing your orchestral work in a short score (for a smaller number of instruments) before orchestrating the music for the full ensemble.
- Solicit recommendations from peers for a copyist to help with parts preparation and score editing.

In this example, the systems-based approach translates the requirements of your goal into actionable steps that also support your overall growth and knowledge acquisition. With this holistic framework in mind, you might also craft a daily or weekly schedule to keep you on track.

Sharing the Vision: Approaching Collaborators

One of the best ways to achieve ambitious objectives is to share your vision with trusted collaborators. They may have a vision that aligns with yours; suddenly, you have a team willing to work with you to make your dream happen. This is how Dale Trumbore and Brandon Elliott decided to collaborate on the album *How to Go On: The Choral Works of Dale Trumbore*: While discussing another project, Elliott mentioned that Choral Arts Initiative was looking to record a major contemporary choral work on their first album. Trumbore shared that she was looking to write a multi-movement secular requiem, and she had already begun collecting the poetry for such a project. Their shared goals had a mutually beneficial outcome, as Choral Arts Initiative would gain a new work to premiere and record, and Trumbore's work would find a new audience through her first full-length choral album.

When you share your vision, and there's a clear alignment with your prospective collaborator, that's your cue to turn the conversation into a collaboration. Effective communication and mutual benefit are the foundations of a successful collaboration, whether it is a multimedia project, a newly commissioned piece, or an album project. When approaching potential collaborators with your vision, be clear about what you need from them and what you can offer in return.

Managing Time and Money within Goal Setting

As your career progresses, you'll likely work on larger-scale projects in addition to smaller ones. Effective time management is crucial for handling multiple projects and long-term goals. Create a schedule that breaks down large tasks into daily or weekly actions. Prioritize your tasks based on these small and large deadlines, and build in plenty of extra time in case your project takes longer than expected.

Long-term projects also require long-term financial planning. As your career develops, you may take on projects with longer timelines, like an opera that will take several years to compose and produce or an album that will take a year to record, edit, mix, master, and release. Just as you would pad a timeline with extra time to meet your deadlines, planning a long-term budget should include allocating contingency funds for unexpected expenses. Ensure that your budget and timeline cover the entire duration of your project, with time and funding to spare. The bigger the project, the more likely it is to require more time or money than initially expected.

All Goals Have a Budget

No matter how abstract, every career goal can be translated into budgetary form. A budget includes not only the direct costs of achieving your goal, but also the time invested and opportunity costs. Breaking down your ambitions into financial terms can help you identify your necessary resources and make a plan to secure them. Even when monetizing the outcome of a goal seems impossible, breaking it down using this process can still provide insight into the feasibility of your goal as you identify potential funding sources and weigh economic factors.

Implementing Basic Economic Principles

You will be more adept at aligning your goals with your artistic, financial, and personal objectives if you can familiarize yourself with a few key economic principles. Learning to allocate your time and resources effectively is a crucial part of a sustainable composing career, and understanding the basics of the following principles can help inform your approach to that decision-making.

Scarcity

The economic principle of scarcity is directly relevant to composers. Scarcity is the basic economic problem that arises because individual resources are limited, but human wants are unlimited. In a composing career, scarcity can manifest as a limited number of multimedia projects, commissioning opportunities, grant funding, or performance slots available in any given year. This can lead to an inherently competitive environment where composers vie for the same limited resources. As a composer, it is crucial to recognize this dynamic so you can strategically plan your career. You can better navigate the challenges posed by scarcity by diversifying your income, cultivating relationships, and strengthening your unique skill set.

Opportunity Cost

Opportunity cost is the value of the alternative you give up when you make a choice. If you spend time practicing the piano instead of composing new music, for example, the opportunity cost is the potential new composition(s) you could have created during that time. All decisions you make—even positive ones—have an opportunity cost.

Sunk Cost

Money or resources that have already been spent and cannot be recovered are considered a sunk cost. If you print one hundred perusal copies of a piece to give away at a conference and only hand out fifty, for instance, the money you paid for those extra unneeded copies is a sunk cost.

Sunk Cost Fallacy

The sunk cost fallacy is the tendency to continue investing in a project or decision based on your cumulative prior investment into that project (in the form of time, money, and/or resources) rather than the current and future benefits. In other words, it's the human tendency to focus on what has already been spent rather than evaluating whether the investment is worth continuing. For example, you invest $1,000 into recording a live concert for an album, then realize the performance you've recorded contains many errors. To avoid the sunk cost fallacy, you would walk away from the recording project (or release a handful of individual tracks as live recordings) rather than spending more money editing and mastering an album you are ultimately unwilling to release.

Cost-Effectiveness

Cost-effectiveness is a measure of how well money or resources are used to achieve a desired outcome. If you choose to hire an assistant for three hours a week at $30 per hour and that frees up more time for you to finish a commission worth thousands of dollars, you've made a cost-effective decision.

Cost-Benefit

Comparing the costs and benefits of an action helps determine its value, known as its cost-benefit. For example, if the cost of buying a new synthesizer for a video game-scoring project is less than the large fee you'll receive to write that music, then the cost-benefit is favorable.

Return on Investment (ROI)

ROI is a measure used to evaluate the efficiency of an investment or to compare the efficiencies of several different investments. For example, calculating the ROI of spending $1,000 to attend a conference can help you decide whether the conference was worth your time and money. If you receive one new commission for $2,000 as a result of networking at the conference, then attending it was a positive return on investment: you've profited by $1,000.

Non-Monetary Value

Non-monetary value is the term for the benefits and satisfaction derived from actions or investments not measurable with a monetary amount, but still providing immeasurable worth. This can include personal fulfillment, human capital, work-life balance, intrinsic reward, professional exposure, skill development, catalog expansion, and reputation building.

For example, you may find that there is no cost-benefit to hiring a recording studio and musicians to make an album, at least in terms of any potential revenue you'll make from album sales. However, the non-monetary value of making the recording—creating lasting relationships as a result of working with those musicians and gaining a fantastic recording that offers proof of your skills—may be well worth the cost of funding that project.

As you set goals for yourself, you'll want to weigh all of the above principles, including non-monetary value. For example, if you value your relationships and artistic growth above monetary gain, your value system will necessarily impact how you structure your long-term ambitions. You might consider moving to an area with a low cost of living, so that you need less money to cover your basic living expenses while prioritizing projects that you find personally meaningful.

All choices come with an opportunity cost. By allocating your time one way, you are necessarily missing out on opportunities you could have gained by spending your time differently. Yet as you establish systems, weigh economic principles, and plan for success, you are setting yourself up for a high return on investment.

Evolving Goals

Goals don't have to be static; in fact, they can and should evolve as you gain experience and your circumstances change. It is important to revisit and adjust your goals periodically, relinquishing those that no longer serve you. Be careful not to fall into a sunk cost fallacy: avoid following through on a vision simply because you've already invested time and resources into that goal.

Not only should your goals evolve over time, but it's also okay to leave yourself a long time span—perhaps much longer than you think you "should" need—to grow your craft as you pursue goals commensurate with your composing. Shawn Kirchner notes that some composers rush to put out their work before they've had a chance to "ripen and grow." His advice for those ambitious composers: "Take your time. Become yourself. Be humble. Have something to say. Learn your craft. Don't be in a hurry to think you're so gloriously wonderful. Become gloriously wonderful over time."

Success often brings new opportunities and challenges. As you achieve your initial goals, take time to redefine what success means to you. Your goals may become more or less ambitious; you may even find that your ambitions shift away from composing and toward another aspect of music or a different career. External factors, like a birth or death, an abrupt shift into a caregiving role, or an unexpected decline in your income, may also necessitate a more forgiving timeline to achieve what you would like to accomplish.

"There is no straight way to success," Miguel del Águila says. "You just have ups and downs, and big ups and big downs. One day you're on top of the world; the next day you hear your music and you're the worst thing you've ever heard." It is impossible, del Águila explains, to expect a career that only trends upward or to make only good career decisions. "The bad decisions you make, and their consequences—they help your music, too. They give you depth."

In the end, del Águila says, he trusts his instinct above all else. He lived in Vienna for a time after pursuing his graduate studies there. When he moved to California, "everybody in Vienna said, 'You must be crazy to go to America. You have a good job. You have the best musicians in the world.'" America, at that time, was in the middle of a crisis, he says, but his instinct told him: "I'm tired of this. I need something new." Others considered the move to be a bad decision, but del Águila disagreed:

> Every decision you make is like a door you open to a new room in your house. It could be the best thing or the worst thing, but how that room is depends on what you do when you get in that room. There are no good or bad decisions; there is just how you make them work for you at that time and afterwards.

Adaptability and continuous reassessment are key to ongoing success as a composer. Consider how your goals shift as you achieve milestones, encounter unforeseen challenges, and navigate new opportunities. Remember that, instead of setting a single fixed goal, you are better off putting a series of systems in place that support your overall development and growth.

When Goals Aren't Necessary or Useful

Rigid goals can sometimes be counterproductive to achieving the kind of success you seek, and goals are not required for artistic fulfillment. Some composers find focusing on a general direction rather than a specific outcome to be more beneficial. Other composers identify strict criteria for what they're seeking in their projects, then allow the work they take on to shape their career. Both approaches allow for greater flexibility than strict goal setting, and both can lead to unexpected composing opportunities.

Molly Joyce intentionally doesn't set goals, as goal setting can feel like a limitation for her creative process and can lead to disappointment. "I don't like to have expectations," she says. "I don't want to feel like I should be at a certain point in five years." Instead of setting goals, she describes her approach as being "open to surprises" as she continues to manifest a life that explores the intersection of music and disability studies within her composition and research.

While Joyce's dual interests in music and disability studies direct her composition path, composers like Kile Smith prefer to work toward a vision—a sort of mission statement that serves as a guiding north star to inform their decisions. "First of all," Smith says, "leaving music out of it, my goal is to make the people around us better. That's what we're here to do. As a composer, I've got to figure out how to make my composing make that happen: make the people around me better." This philosophy extends into Smith's process, informing the way he writes each new piece:

> I think so often composers get in their heads, "This is the sound that I want, and these [performers] are going to do that. They're going to make that sound." And I don't think that way. I want to write something that is going to allow them to bloom. . . . It may sound very grandiose that I want to make this gift to them, but that's really what I do. I think that's what we're here on earth to do.

For Smith, composing is a chance to let performers be "the musicians that they ought to be, that they want to be, [and] that they aspire to be." In other words, commissions are a chance to serve musicians—to embrace their skills and let them shine. This philosophy guides all of Smith's work.

Identify Your Guiding Principles

Consider crafting your own mission statement. Why do you create music? As a composer, you hone your craft; you might aspire to find an audience, big or small, that loves your art. You might hope this craft will also support you financially and artistically in a sustainable way, creating a career that will last decades, or a lifetime. You'll be more likely to thrive long-term, without burning out, if you have a strong motivation for *why* you do this work. You can approach that question from a business perspective: "Why should anyone spend money on my music?" Or you can approach it from a creative or even spiritual one, returning to questions like these: "What good am I creating with the art that I make?" "What value am I adding to the world?" "How am I helping others and contributing to my community?"

Your answers will create a mission statement to guide your career. Like Smith, you may use your music as a tool to showcase the best aspects of every musician who performs your work. You may compose because writing music is the best way you know to advocate for justice. You may write music because it lets you work through the darkest and most complex emotions that humans feel. You may create art because doing so allows you, your performers, and your audience to come out the other side of those dark emotions feeling healed in some way.

No matter what the lodestar for your composition may be, keeping that ultimate purpose in mind will allow you to hold ambitions driven by purpose and meaning, not just short-term gain. That purpose allows you to set goals and take on projects that align with your values—or, like Joyce, to eschew goals altogether and pursue the work and research you find most meaningful. Create systems that allow you to grow as an artist and a human—systems that also see you recognizing and enriching the community around you. If you establish strong systems around your ambitions, it matters less whether you attain a specific metric of success. With systems that allow for artistic, personal, and community growth, you'll be better off for having pursued your work regardless of if, or when, you reach your goals.

5

Establishing a Strong Foundation

How do you transition to thinking of yourself as a professional and act accordingly? Professional composers look for ways to invest in themselves to make their jobs easier. These investments can come in the form of free resources, lessons or coaching, equipment upgrades, hiring assistance, investing in your health, or creating high-quality recordings of your work. As with a financial investment, any efforts you put into your career early on can compound over time. This chapter takes a close look at the many ways to invest in yourself and your music, whether you are early in your career or more established.

Free Resources

Even without money, you can find free resources to help you along your path. Composers wishing to learn more about orchestration might self-educate by way of online videos about how to compose for different instruments as well as websites devoted to exploring each instrument's extended techniques. Many graduate schools offer scholarships and teaching stipends to composers who can teach music theory and aural skills. Can you brush up on your theory knowledge using free resources like online videos and library books to give yourself a greater chance of attending graduate school on a paid teaching assistantship?

If your only currency is time, you can still find ways to nurture your career. Can you find paid work in grant writing or assisting another composer, so that you are getting paid while learning skills that will enhance your own career? Can you barter your skills to gain the experience you seek, offering teaching or tutoring hours rather than paying with money?

The best free investments you can make in any composing career are experience—honing your craft—and relationship building. Reaching out to prospective collaborators with cold or "warm" messages, as discussed in Chapter 2, is free. For many composers, time spent working with collaborators is the best way to learn how to compose. In Dale Trumbore's experience, real-life collaborations with musicians are a better "teacher" than any composition

Composing a Living. Brandon Elliott and Dale Trumbore, Oxford University Press.
© Brandon Elliott and Dale Trumbore 2025. DOI: 10.1093/9780197803509.003.0006

lesson, and working one on one with instrumentalists yields longer-lasting knowledge than any orchestration class.

The $5,000 Question

In the interviews for this book, two questions in particular unlocked a wealth of information on how composers would prioritize building their career:

- "Knowing what you know now, if you suddenly got a check for $5,000 and it had to be invested into you and your craft, how would you use the money?"
- "When you do have extra funds to use toward your career, what's the best investment?"

The composers featured here gave a variety of answers for these questions, with several composers noting that they would have given a different answer for every prior stage of their career. Their answers differed depending on whether the composer was looking to create a stronger portfolio, make music with excellent tools and software, or prioritize their health and well-being through childcare, therapy, and paying off medical bills. Even with a diverse range of answers, we found that composers' answers fit into the following categories.

Lessons, Coaching or Schooling

Composers who recalled the earliest stages of their composing sometimes wished they'd spent more time honing their craft. Obtaining an undergraduate or graduate degree in music composition can not only strengthen your skills but also introduce you to a network of close and potentially lifelong collaborators. Investing your time and money into private lessons—or bartering another skill in exchange for those lessons—can also help develop your craft.

Zanaida Stewart Robles notes that, at this more established point in her career, she's happy to invest money into coaching sessions and lessons to gain feedback and advice on her compositions. But she's also likely to reach out to friends and colleagues for more casual feedback, an option open to any composer regardless of budget. As discussed in Chapter 2, building a network of composer-peers can be just as important as networking with potential collaborators.

Equipment and Software

If you primarily compose instrumental works, particularly larger or electronic works such as film or video game scores, orchestral works, or pieces for wind ensemble, consider investing in a good sample library. That said, sample libraries and composing software—from notation programs to digital audio workstations (DAWs)—can be expensive. Many of these programs offer a monthly subscription-based payment option, which may be more financially accessible to beginning composers. Several composers we interviewed also mentioned free sample libraries. If you are still a student, consider taking advantage of student discounts to save on equipment and software while you can. (See the Resources section for examples of free sample libraries and software options.)

Many of the composers we interviewed said their top priority, now, would be investing in great instruments or software. Juhi Bansal said she would put an unexpected $5,000 check toward a new hybrid digital piano, whereas several other composers mentioned buying a top-tier sample library. If you compose for digital media, using a DAW and maintaining a decent sound library will be essential to your work. But how do you decide when to purchase new gear?

"I am of two minds on this, because you can definitely spend a lot of money on both hardware and software," Isaac Io Schankler says. If media composers aren't careful, they can easily overspend on audio plugins, synthesizers, and sound libraries. Schankler acknowledges that investing in some of these resources may be necessary as you build your body of work; for example, they recently purchased a new clarinet sample library with a specific composition in mind. Still, "don't buy it just to buy it," Schankler says. "I try to be careful about my purchases, but there's still stuff I just never ended up using. There's a synthesizer sitting next to me right now that I don't think I've ever plugged in." Purchasing new software, hardware, or a new sound library makes the most sense when you know you're going to use it for a specific project.

Conferences and Concerts

"I can't think of anything that's been more beneficial to my career year after year than showing up at various conferences," Alex Shapiro says. "That was how I got a lot of balls rolling. . . . A lot of people already knew me from social media, but that in-person [connection] was huge." She suggests that composers invest money in making face-to-face connections that can, over time, foster new collaborations. "Composers should earmark the money they would have otherwise foolishly spent on submission fees to competitions that they're unlikely to win, nor which are designed to foster a meaningful professional relationship, and instead use that money to fund the expenses of attending conferences and concerts."

Website Design and Maintenance

A web presence is so important for composers, and building that presence may involve hiring outside help. That said, many composers build their own websites, especially when budget is a concern. On your website, include a catalog of your works with links to purchase those works, even if that "link to purchase" is simply your contact page. Along with a downloadable high-resolution headshot, a bio, and as many good-quality live recordings of your work as possible, make it explicitly clear on your website how potential collaborators can reach you if they're interested in collaborating.

Hired Personnel or Management

Several composers noted that they would use extra, unexpected income to hire an assistant or manager. In doing so, they would free up time they'd spend answering emails or negotiating commissioning contracts, leaving them with more time for their composition. Angélica Negrón says she would use an extra $5,000 in part to hire help with writing grants; this decision could, in turn, secure even more funding. Abbie Betinis notes that, while her priorities for any unexpected income have shifted over the years, a top priority now is putting that money toward childcare—an expense that parents would likely agree counts as both hired assistance and an investment toward their mental health.

Financial Investments and Paying Down Debt

Earlier in Betinis's career, her rule was that "all surprise money, like competition prizes or even ASCAP royalties, which you never count on" all went to pay down her mortgage. "Anything I haven't budgeted for, it goes to my highest loan, along with the highest interest rate, which happened to be my mortgage." Prioritizing paying down her mortgage allowed her first home purchase, ten years later, to become an investment property. "It's a side hustle," she says. "I'm a landlord for that property, and that mortgage is going to be gone in five years. So that means with the renters in there constantly, which has been great, that mortgage has paid for itself for the last fifteen years of its life."

Reena Esmail and Timothy C. Takach also recommend using any un-expected income or grants to pay off outstanding debts, particularly credit cards, which often charge exorbitant interest rates. In a composing career, that debt can sometimes occur in the form of travel expenses—like flights or hotel costs—for which you haven't yet been reimbursed.

Health: Mental and Physical Well-Being

Mari Esabel Valverde notes that, alongside other self-investment goals men-tioned here, like funding a recording project, she'd also prioritize investing $5,000 in her well-being. "I feel like I would be more successful in my career if I were in good mental health [and] if I were able to access the resources that I need to finish my transition and be one with my body," she says. "There are things I would use that money for before my career." If you neglect your mental and physical well-being, it becomes exponentially harder to write music. Composing may feel like your top priority in life, especially as you ap-proach a deadline, but your health takes precedence over everything else.

Recordings: Producing Albums, Live Recordings, and Demos

By far, the most common answer composers gave to the "$5,000 question" was that recording is probably the best way to invest in your career. "If I were a young composer, I would be throwing all my resources at getting killer recordings," Eric Whitacre says. "If a recording of your music gives you chills, you can hope that it'll give other people chills, and then people are going to want to replicate that" by programming and performing that work. Without recordings, it can be infinitely more difficult to convince a conductor, en-semble, or solo performer to program your work. A good recording serves as both "proof of concept"—this piece can successfully be performed, and this piece is worth performing—as well as an indication that you've suc-cessfully navigated working relationships and are capable of collaborating professionally.

Shara Nova has recorded several rock albums through her band My Brightest Diamond, but she wishes she had invested more into her classical recordings. "Because a lot of my classical compositions were based on live performances, and there are very few recordings of those concerts or that material, in many ways, it's almost as if it doesn't exist," she says of her earliest works. Nova observes that some colleagues who also create both commercial and concert music and who have focused on making recordings of their concert work have found greater success than those, like Nova, who haven't prioritized classical recordings. Nova has no regrets, she says, but at this point in her life, she wants to "prioritize getting those recordings made, so that there is more documentation of the work."

The Cost of Recording

For many composers, investing in high-quality recordings has been crucial to their success. However, as Mari Esabel Valverde notes, the cost of professional recording sessions is often prohibitively high, which can prevent composers from creating albums. "There are so many excellent musicians," Valverde says, "so many budding composers, so many creative people doing interesting, important work that needs to be heard, that hasn't been heard."

Smaller albums, like those only featuring soloists or small chamber ensembles, may be produced for a budget of about $5,000 each. However, larger ensembles may budget $10,000–50,000 or higher—even upward of $100,000—to produce an album. Ensembles of professional musicians will inherently cost substantially more than volunteer ensembles. Most classical albums will never break even, let alone earn a profit, which means that both you and your collaborating ensemble must perceive an inherent nonmonetary value to any recording project—a reason to pursue the project even knowing that it won't generate income. While there are grants available specific to the creation of new recordings, grant funding for composers in the United States can be limited, depending on your state and local resources. Still, there are creative ways to reduce costs while capturing great recordings of your compositions.

If you are still in school or teach at a university with a recording program and/or studio, consider utilizing those resources while you have the chance. If you live in an area that has local or regional grants specific to recordings, apply every time you are eligible. Some composers recruit friends who volunteer their time to record, which can significantly reduce expenses. While professionally produced recordings are the gold standard for composers, consider adding a clause to your commissioning contracts to specify that you'll receive a live audio and/or video recording of your premiere to use for self-promotional, non-commercial purposes. While the live recording may not be as high-quality as a studio recording, it can still be incredibly valuable in representing your work on your website. Whether it is a professionally produced or live recording, having *any* recording of an actual ensemble performing your concert music—as opposed to a computer-generated demo—adds social proof to the feasibility and appeal of your music.

Miguel del Águila agrees that live recordings can be a much more cost-effective investment than studio recordings. On a quality scale of 1–100, he says, a live recording of a piece may be a 70, whereas a note-perfect studio recording of that piece might be a 99—but the studio recording could cost you $10,000 to record. The cost may not be worth the investment, both for monetary reasons and because studio recordings sometimes lack the verve that live recordings capture. "Music needs the adrenaline of a performance," he says. "Music needs the performer knowing that a difficult passage approaches and that adrenaline is helping the music be more powerful and exciting." He thinks it is smart to first see what you get for your money—or for free—if you make a good live recording with good musicians before you take the same musicians to a recording studio.

Recordings are very important to del Águila because they are "what remains" of your work. As concert-attending audiences decline, recordings become even more crucial. They also offer proof of how to best perform your music long after a concert is over. "Whenever I write a new piece, I'm desperate for the first recording," del Águila says. "Until musicians have a model of a performance, your music is at risk, because it depends on who plays it next and the level of talent. Once there is a recording, you [can] tell them, 'Go on Spotify, listen to this, and it will give you an idea.' So to me, the recording is always very important."

As a composer, you can leverage the non-monetary value of professional recordings in negotiations. For example, if an ensemble approaches you for a commission and the fee is typically lower than you would accept, but they are open to the idea of creating a professional recording of your work, the collective "package deal" of your commission contract increases in value substantially. Similarly, if they offer you a substantial commissioning fee that is typically higher than you would accept, you could consider asking if they'd be open to the possibility of allocating some of those funds toward a professional recording.

Creating Live and Demo Recordings

Some of the interviewed composers found it helpful, at the start of their careers, to put together a concert of their work with friends performing for free or a minimal fee. These composers invested in high-quality audio and video recordings of the concert, which they later used online and in competition and grant applications. If you pursue this strategy, consider sharing the concert with one or more composer colleagues and splitting the performance and recording costs.

For Thomas Kotcheff, the value of making a recording has changed from needing representations of his work to wanting to create an artifact of various projects and concerts. He saw a marked change in his career once his piano duo HOCKET started making recordings. "On our first big concert we gave, I said [to HOCKET duo partner Sarah Gibson], 'Sarah, we need to have three cameras here, and we've got to put down $1,000 to make a really good video performance of this concert.' And we did, and that made a massive difference." While it's one thing to be performing a lot in concert, Kotcheff notes, it's another to have plentiful recordings online where people can find your music.

Many composers have found that even a brief or less-polished live representation of their work is preferable to a computer-generated demo of that work. This is particularly true with vocal music, where sound libraries still have trouble replicating the nuances of live voices. If you are having trouble pulling together a performance of your work, consider recruiting friends or colleagues for a one-hour reading session. Even a polished one- or two-minute demo of a vocal work might offer a more compelling representation than a computer-generated one.

Many composers have created recordings of their work at low or no cost. Their strategies included performing their own work, trading a commission in exchange for a performer recording the work professionally, or relying on a school's resources as a student or professor, using discounted or free recording space and access to the school's student or professional recording engineers. Even with no money, you could use or borrow a phone or laptop to record yourself or a group of friends performing your music.

If you are a composer-performer, like Zanaida Stewart Robles and many of the other composers we interviewed, you have the option to create your own recordings. When Robles realized she didn't have good recordings for the choral compositions she most believed in, she recorded them herself. "A lot of my Soundcloud [portfolio] is me overdubbing myself," she says. "It's just a fun pastime. My recordings [are] not commercial recordings, but they're good enough to give you a sense of what the piece sounds like." Now, further along in her path, Robles is seeking out higher-quality, professional-level recordings of her work. Still, those initial recordings made in GarageBand helped conductors and performers find her work and hear how to perform it. Making the recordings didn't cost Robles anything except her time and the price of her computer, which came with GarageBand already installed.

Self-Produced Recordings

Dale Trumbore has self-produced three albums for a budget of about $5,000 each, using a mix of crowdfunding and savings. For the first of these albums, her 2011 release *Snow White Turns Sixty*, she and soprano Gillian Hollis crowdfunded $4,202 on Kickstarter to put toward album recording costs. Trumbore's savings contributed approximately $1,000 more to complete the album and pay Hollis. Trumbore's 2024 albums *The Gleam* and *She Only Remembers* were funded through her business, using income from commissioning and score sales royalties. On each album, Trumbore also performed as a pianist.

While most recording engineers charge an hourly rate for recording, editing, mixing, and mastering, Trumbore's recording engineer for *The Gleam* and *She Only Remembers* charged an all-inclusive set rate per day, which covered not only daily recording costs, but also the fees for later editing, mixing, and mastering the recording sessions. Trumbore recorded these two thirty-minute albums—one for soprano, piano, and clarinet, the other for solo piano—in the span of three days. Additional album costs came from renting the concert hall in which she recorded, paying performers, licensing the photography used for both albums, hiring a graphic designer, and distributing the finished album.

While self-producing a recording project gives you complete creative control over the finished result, it also generates expensive problems that only you can solve. As in Trumbore's example above, in self-producing an album, you are solely responsible for creating and sticking to a budget, planning a realistic timeline, finding a recording space and recording engineer(s), contracting out your musicians and additional producer(s), hiring a graphic designer and/or licensing album art, and managing the logistics of distributing and promoting your album.

A great way to collect recommendations for a recording studio and engineer is to ask your peers and colleagues. Note that you'll want an engineer who has experience recording your genre of music. For example, if you are recording a choral album, you'll want an engineer who has experience working with vocalists. On the other hand, an engineer who works primarily with singers may not be your first pick for an album of music for percussion quartet and electronics. Luckily, most recording engineers have a wide breadth of experience that will serve you well.

You may choose to have your recording engineer master the album or use a separate mastering engineer. Consider, too, whether you'll produce your recording sessions or hire someone else to produce them. A session producer serves as an extra set of ears, noting whether you need to record another take or are ready to move on. Your session producer will also take notes throughout the recording process, observing which takes were more successful than others. These notes can be crucial later in the editing process, when you are picking the best takes and deciding how to edit them together.

Performing on your own album can cut costs, as can serving as your own producer. However, it can be challenging to perform both roles simultaneously. While it is technically possible to produce a session while performing, this makes each job much harder to do well. If you are performing on a recording alongside other musicians, for instance, it can be difficult to grasp subtle mistakes in their parts while also keeping track of your own errors. Even if you are recording as a solo performer, it is virtually impossible to also track and transcribe the detailed notes for each take that you will need while editing. If you are not performing on your own album, though, you may choose to produce it yourself or co-produce with someone else. If you *are* performing on your album, consider bringing in a session producer, whether that means paying a colleague or finding a friend willing to volunteer their time in exchange for an album producer credit.

Be prepared for any self-produced recording project to go over budget and take longer than expected. Your engineer may run into delays in editing and mixing the album. Your graphic designer may need an extra week—or month—to finish your design. You may run over budget and need to fundraise to cover unexpected additional costs. It is always easier to allot extra money and time and not end up needing them than it is to bump up against unexpected delays or expenses and have to postpone your album release.

The following list of questions will serve you well as you begin to plan a self-produced recording project. If you take time to plan your project carefully, you'll be better-equipped for any delays that arise later in the recording process.

- Why is it essential that you make this recording now?
- How will the recording serve your career?
- What is the budget for the project?
  - How are you going to fund the album?

- If you are anticipating using grant funding for the album but those grants fall through, what are other ways you could fund the project?
- If you are crowdfunding the project, what incentives will you provide to those backing this album?
- If you are using savings to cover full or partial costs for the project, are you financially prepared to go over budget?
- Whom are you planning to hire for the project?
- Are you performing on the album?
- Will you hire an additional producer for the album, or will you produce it yourself?
- What will the album art be?
  - Will you hire a graphic designer for the album art?
  - Will you license photography or stage a photoshoot to generate art for the album?
- What's the timeline for the project?
  - Have you factored in extra time in case each stage of the process takes longer than expected?
  - What is the anticipated release date for the project?
- How will you promote and distribute the project when it is done?

Distribution: Physical and Digital

With current distribution models, it has never been easier to self-release an album for a minimal budget. Options for self-distributing albums continue to evolve, but most platforms simply require you to upload your high-resolution audio tracks and album art, manually input track information and album credits (also known as metadata), enter your release date, and pay a relatively low fee. (See the Resources section for several distribution options for self-releasing albums.)

While the musical landscape has shifted heavily toward streaming and digital platforms, there is still a small market for physical distribution. The music industry has seen a spike in both vinyl and CD options, and industry experts attribute this to the human desire to have a tangible connection to the music that resonates with them. For many years, having a physical distribution element was required to make a classical album eligible for Billboard charting; however, with the rise of digital-only releases, this rule is likely to change.

To be clear, Billboard charting is not essential to the success of an album. However, it can generate notable attention. Typically, a charting album will experience a second wave of purchases and streams, albeit one smaller than the initial release. This subsequent wave effect usually occurs each week that the album charts. Charting can also draw the attention of radio stations or review outlets, including ones who might have dismissed your initial pitch. All three of Brandon Elliott's albums with his ensemble Choral Arts Initiative have charted. In each case, he found that once the album charted, someone who initially declined to review the album changed their mind and decided to write a review. Physical sales and streams also enjoyed an additional upward trend.

For a self-produced album, once you have your physical album's corresponding Universal Product Code (UPC), you can submit your metadata to Luminate (formerly Nielsen SoundScan) to make your album eligible to chart on Billboard. Luminate is the organization that tracks consumer data for all music products, and they provide that data to Billboard to tabulate charting. All of this is typically unnecessary if your album is being distributed with a label; they will usually handle such matters, though it never hurts to have these details spelled out clearly in your agreement with the label.

Working with a Label vs. Forming Your Own Imprint

The music industry has changed significantly over the last few decades, and record labels are no exception. Gone are the days when labels would cover all the expenses related to the creation of a new recording. Now, in the classical music space, you would typically approach a label after an album is "in the can" (industry jargon for "ready to release"). The label will not reimburse or realize any expenses related to the creation of your recordings. The appeal of working with a label lies in their marketing prowess: their ability to distribute your music, design the cover and liner notes (though you'll typically need to provide all of the print-ready text), generate press coverage, and drive sales. Some classical labels may even charge you a fee for these services, further underscoring the question of whether it is valuable to partner with a label. Additionally, almost all labels will collect a majority of sales proceeds, with the remaining profits distributed to you or any other copyright holders.

Forming your own record label or label imprint—a subdivision of your company—can be a simple process. There is nothing you need to get started; whether or not you are incorporated, you can make the record label or label imprint part of your existing business. As with self-publishing, the appeal of forming your own label is that you have direct control over all aspects of the album and its release. However, just as with self-publishing, your control comes with the trade-offs discussed earlier: it takes a great deal of time, effort, and money to self-produce and self-distribute an album.

Marketing and Publicity

Generating attention for your new recording release is just as challenging as generating attention for anything you create: it takes planning, strategy, consistent execution, and, in many cases, repetition. The below steps can generate publicity for your album. Keep in mind, though, that funding for arts journalism and public radio continues to decline, and reviews are harder than ever to receive.

- First, examine your current network and see if you know anyone affiliated with local, school, or regional radio. Even if you don't have personal connections to these radio stations, it can still be worth reaching out about your album.
- Second, make a list of press connections to contact about the upcoming release, including reporters for newspapers, magazines, and online music outlets, as well as individual reviewers. As with radio, you'll have more luck reaching out to press contacts if you already have an established connection, but don't let that stop you.
- Third, create a compelling press release that includes direct links to preview or download the master recording(s) along with all assets related to the album (cover art, liner notes, etc.). It is easy to find templates online with a standard formula for an album press release, or you could also use artificial intelligence to generate one with the details of your release, making sure to proofread, revise, and expand it before you send it out.
- Fourth, prepare to send out your press release as an email. Write a brief introduction, followed by your press release copied into the body of the email. Include either links to download your album alongside other assets (e.g., liner notes, artist bios, etc.) or a link to a website where the album and assets can be easily accessed through streaming or downloads. As with cold emails, send your work as links, not attachments; your message will be less likely to be flagged as spam and deleted. If you've created a physical album as well as a digital one, consider mailing physical copies of your album to the radio stations on your list. While this is increasingly less necessary, as many stations now rely on digital assets rather than hard-copy albums, some radio stations still prefer this practice.

Alongside these more traditional album-promotion tactics, consider sending out an album announcement to your friends, family, and colleagues. You may want to split this up into an announcement about the album before the release—ideally with the option to pre-order or pre-save the album—alongside an announcement on the actual release date. You'll likely also want to post about your album on social media, sharing not only the release but also the behind-the-scenes work of recording it. Consider sharing interviews, any positive media coverage of your album, inclusion on notable playlists or radio broadcasts, or information about the album charting on Billboard or another distribution platform. You may also consider hiring a publicist for the promotion of your album, though you may find the high cost of retaining a publicist is not worth the expense. (Chapter 8 will address the pros and cons of hiring a publicist to promote your work.)

Getting a spontaneous check for $5,000 may sound unlikely. Still, some composers find unexpected payments arriving—sometimes in large amounts—in the form of larger-than-usual performing rights payments, for example, or an unanticipated grant win. Even if you don't receive a surprise inheritance or win a MacArthur Fellowship, these self-investment ideas provide a roadmap for where your money is best put to use, whether that's $50 or $5,000.

Investing time and money into your well-being and craft builds the foundation for a thriving career, but the next step is just as essential: understanding the value of your work. As the following chapter explores how to effectively price your work, you will learn how to assign monetary value to the art you create. A clear and confident approach to pricing your music ensures that the time, effort, and expertise you have invested into your craft are reflected in what you earn.

6
Pricing Your Work

Composers face several pricing decisions. The rates you charge are linked to your developing sense of self-worth, which is why it's important to develop a strong sense of the value of your time and the inherent worth of your music early on in your career. Perhaps one of the hardest financial transitions for a composer is moving from working for free to charging for your work. That transition comes with several challenges:

- How do you talk confidently about money in conversations with collaborators and peers?
- How do you determine the price of your commissions, score sales, and speaking gigs?
- How do you know when it's time to raise your rates?
- When, if ever, should you work for free again?

This chapter will discuss how to navigate all the above questions. Different composers have different ways of assigning value to their work, and with practice, you'll arrive at the pricing and negotiation strategies that work best for you.

Talking Confidently about Money

Bringing up the topic of money can be challenging, whether you are assessing a collaborator's commissioning budget or trying to assess what rates your peers or mentors are charging. Many composers are uncomfortable talking about their rates, especially at the start of their careers. This discomfort could stem from several reasons: maybe you are insecure about the rates you are currently charging, and you are afraid to name a number because you worry you are over- or undervaluing your worth. Conversations about money require a degree of vulnerability; maybe you are conflict- and competition-averse, or you are a very private person who doesn't like talking about finances.

Composing a Living. Brandon Elliott and Dale Trumbore, Oxford University Press.
© Brandon Elliott and Dale Trumbore 2025. DOI: 10.1093/9780197803509.003.0007

Understanding the root cause of your discomfort can help challenge your assumptions about money in conversation and inform what you *are* willing to share. You are far from alone in your unease; remember that most people feel the same way about discussing money, at least at first. However, these discussions are worthwhile for your benefit and for the good of your profession. You may have heard the platitude that a "rising tide lifts all boats." Conversations about finances can lift all *rates*, resulting in more equitable pay.

Conversations about money may require practice and a willingness to overcome your initial discomfort. Luckily, as a musician, you are already well prepared to practice your way through an unfamiliar challenge. Each new conversation about a potential commission brings another opportunity to practice your negotiating skills.

Even after you've overcome your own discomfort, though, you may find that others are squeamish about discussing concrete numbers. No matter how well you know a friend or colleague, asking someone what they charge—for commissioning fees, for residencies and clinics, or for other gigs—can be perceived as rude, uncouth, or aggressively direct. But if directly asking how much a friend or colleague charges can lead to an uncomfortable relationship, how are you supposed to find out how much your peers are charging for their work?

With close friends, you may find that bringing up the rates you currently charge—a conversation that does require a degree of vulnerability—may result in your friend voluntarily sharing their own rates. Dale Trumbore has a few specific friends with whom these conversations flow easily and effortlessly. She has known these colleagues for years; these are relationships built on mutual respect and comfortable vulnerability. Trumbore and her colleagues discuss their finances so that they'll all be paid more fairly and equitably in the future.

These colleague-friendships don't always come easily or quickly, and you may be wondering how to price your work if you have yet to form those close relationships. Your mentors and teachers may also be hesitant to discuss money, although some of the composers interviewed did cite mentors who generously shared their own rates. In any case, there's one sentence you can ask any colleague, mentor, or professor, when asking "What would you charge for this project?" feels uncomfortably direct. Instead of asking what someone else would charge, say: "What do you think I should charge for this project?"

A mentor, teacher, or other colleague who is reluctant to discuss their own rates will probably be much more open about giving their advice on what you should or could charge. In doing so, they'll likely reveal either what they would charge now for the same service or what they would have charged when they were where you are now. With that question in hand, you can get virtually anyone's opinion on what price you should quote for a project. Whether you are researching prices on your own or weighing the opinions of your colleagues, remember that different composers set different rates for their work. Not only that, but they may also have different—and strong!—opinions on how to set their rates. This strategy can be used to inquire about any kind of project that involves flexible rates, like commissions, recordings, clinics, residencies, synchronization licensing, or other fees.

As you become more established in your career, you'll have more power to shape how composers discuss money. You may feel compelled to share information about your finances in the name of creating a more transparent culture around music and business. That's a wonderful instinct, and we encourage you to do so. Before you do, you may find it helpful to consider your boundaries around what you feel comfortable sharing privately or publicly.

Some composers are more comfortable sharing past rates than current ones—for example, what their total composing income was two years ago. Others are more comfortable sharing exactly what they charge now. If you are bluntly asked to share a rate and doing so crosses a personal boundary, consider the inverse of the question mentioned above: "While I'm not comfortable sharing what I charge now, I would charge this amount if I was in your position." Transparent conversations around money in music lead to a fairer industry. Share as often and as much information as you are comfortable sharing, and pay your knowledge forward.

Negotiating Effectively

When negotiating a fee, Molly Joyce always tries to get the other person to throw out a number first. "Sometimes they might propose a higher fee than you'd ever dreamed of," she says. This is one of the most common and useful pieces of advice given about negotiation, and it certainly applies to commission pricing.

Frank Ticheli had to learn this lesson through personal experience. "I remember I got a commission from someone I respected a lot," he says. "He asked, 'Well, how much do you think is a fair price?'" Ticheli offered a number that the commissioner quickly accepted. "I realized then that maybe it's not always the best thing for the composer to volunteer the commission fee," he says, "because I could tell by the way he answered that he was prepared to pay me at least double the amount that I spit out. That was a huge lesson."

If asking the other person to name a number feels uncomfortable at first, try asking, "What does your budget look like for this project?" When you know your potential collaborator has commissioned music previously, you could also ask, "What has compensation looked like for similar projects in the past?" Many composers feel intimidated by negotiation, even well into their professional careers. Like any muscle, though, this skill becomes easier the more you exercise it.

Brandon Elliott notes that some artistic and executive directors won't offer you a higher fee once you've thrown out a low number. From a business perspective, it is in their best interest to accept your low rate. If Elliott's ensemble, Choral Arts Initiative (CAI), approaches a composer about a commission and the composer suggests a low commissioning fee, Elliott's response may differ depending on his relationship with the person in his role as the business executive of a nonprofit organization. If he knows the composer personally, he'll often say, "This higher amount is what we paid the last composer for a very similar situation; you might want to consider this amount instead." On one occasion, when a composer offered a very low commissioning rate, CAI compensated them further by offering an additional stipend to workshop the piece with the ensemble—an expense CAI doesn't usually cover.

On the other end of the spectrum, if a composer quotes an exceptionally high rate, Elliott views that not as a "no," but as a "not now." He thanks them for sharing their rate, notes that the ensemble has their information on file, and says—genuinely—that as soon as they have the budgetary means to fund that commission, they'll be in touch. In other words, he doesn't think: "Oh, this person is charging way more than they're worth," but rather: "This person is charging what they think they're worth. We can't afford it yet, but we'll wait until we get to that point, and there's no harm." There are no hard feelings on either end.

Think of negotiation from a purely business perspective: Once you have offered a low commissioning rate, your room for negotiation on the price has vanished. It is in the commissioner's best interest to accept a low rate when one is offered. For this reason, consider quoting rates that you feel great about, or even rates that feel slightly high.

When a potential commissioner approaches Kile Smith to ask for his rate, Smith avoids using the word "you" in the resulting conversation. "It can be taken as very personalizing and very confrontational if you say 'you,'" Smith explains, in phrases like, "I want *you* to do this." Instead of asking "What are you going to pay?" Smith suggests you talk instead about your commissioner's budget. By using the phrase "the budget," you position yourself on the same side as the negotiating party. You are both trying to figure out and work within a shared budget. "It just reduces all the tension," Smith says. This way, you are both working toward the best possible result. Keep in mind, too, that the person with whom you are having this conversation may be dealing with the same pressure and potential confusion around pricing that you are feeling.

As you progress in your career, especially if you are still uncomfortable discussing commissioning rates, consider having an assistant or manager take on those conversations for you. Derrick Skye once agreed to a commissioning fee that he felt was far below what was acceptable. It was at that moment that he realized it would be best to remove himself from the equation when there were discussions regarding money, especially when negotiating with a friend or colleague. He now has a manager who handles conversations about money. (Chapter 8 will further discuss the role that managers and assistants can play in your career.)

Pricing Commissions

In a composing career, you will likely need to determine prices for your commissions, individual scores, rehearsal visits (virtual and/or in-person), and licensing fees. Commissioning rates may be determined by the length of a piece, its instrumentation (or number of total staves), or the approximate number of hours it will take to write the piece. (Chapter 10 will discuss common terms of commissioning contracts, including project timelines, rights and exclusivity periods, and payment structures, in more detail.)

Mari Esabel Valverde calculates her commissioning fees based on the approximate number of minutes of a finished composition. That rate "used to be $1,000 per minute no matter what it was," she says. Now, her rate varies depending on ensemble size.

It is common for composers to determine a commissioning fee by instrumentation and length in addition to a per-minute rate. A piece for a soloist, for example, could cost $500/minute, while a piece for chorus or small ensemble could cost $1,000/minute. A piece for a larger ensemble, like wind ensemble or orchestra, might be closer to $2,000/minute. These numbers are, of course, only examples. At the start of a career, many composers will accept lower rates; your rates increase as your experience grows.

Valverde notes that composers calculating fees should consider not only composing time, but the total time involved in other factors of a commission. These could include communicating with the ensemble, obtaining copyright permission for a text and paying any fees associated with that copyright, sketching a piece, engraving, and editing. The relationship between time and money is inherently complex in art, Valverde says, in part because the line between work and life blurs. "I'm always working on my composition," Valverde says. "Whatever my commission is, I'm going to bed thinking about it. I'm waking up thinking about it." For that reason, it's helpful to have set rates in mind that account for the total time a project will take.

Julia Adolphe initially began tracking her composing hours not with pricing in mind, but rather with the goal of understanding how long it takes her to write a piece. With that information, she figured she could schedule her commissioning work and other projects appropriately, knowing she had enough time to complete each piece. "It takes me 19.5 [composing] hours per minute of orchestral music," she says, "and I don't know why, but the last three pieces have averaged exactly to that." She acknowledges that she may spend more time than others on her composing. With a target rate of at least $100 an hour in mind, Adolphe uses her total anticipated composing hours to calculate an adequate fee.

Jake Runestad's philosophy on score pricing is similar to Adolphe's. Since there aren't standardized rates for commissioning fees, Runestad notes, it takes research and experience to determine them:

> I learned from composer Libby Larsen that it's helpful to calculate fees for rehearsals, residencies, and commissions based on hourly rates (when possible). Though it's difficult to determine how many hours it takes to write a piece of music (given the countless hours of subconscious processing), a rough calculation of an hourly rate is a useful metric. Also, I have a circle of trusted colleagues that help when I have questions about these kinds of fees. One's rates should be reassessed regularly to gauge the value of each income stream and how they relate to one's financial needs, economic inflation, or other external factors. As one's popularity grows, they have the ability to be more selective with their projects and to adjust their rates accordingly.

In addition to pricing per minute of music written or pricing by total composing hours, some composers calculate commissioning fees a third way, considering the number of total staff lines in a piece. This is a similar approach to determining a rate based on instrumentation, like quoting a different fee for an orchestral project versus a choral work. However, this approach accounts for more flexibility when writing for two-staff instruments (e.g., piano or marimba) and chamber ensembles of varying sizes. Kile Smith employs this method, and begins by counting up the number of staff lines in the score:

So if it's a church anthem, let's say SATB, that's four [staves], and if they want organ, I'm going to count three for organ unless they just want a very simple organ [part], so make that two. So that becomes six times the number of minutes. So if it's three minutes, that's eighteen [staves], and then I go eighteen times the number in my head, and then I come up with something. However, there's a lot of wiggle room there. . . . What I'll do is I'll say, "Well, this is what I've gotten in the past," and I'll give them a range. It might be a small range, or it might be a large range.

Note that charging a per-minute rate is often an internal calculation you perform *before* quoting your rate to a prospective collaborator. In concert music, you may find that if you quote your per-minute rate to a commissioner who has initially approached you about writing a ten-minute or longer piece, they may backtrack and ask about having you compose a shorter work. Many composers calculate their commissioning rate, then present that rate to the commissioner, saying something like, "My rate is about $10,000 for a piece of that instrumentation and length." If you are willing to be flexible, you might say something like, "My rate has been approximately $8,000–10,000 for a piece of that scope." With this approach, though, most collaborators will ignore the higher end of your range and offer the lower number. A better tactic is to ask a commissioner their budget before you are asked to reveal yours. Later in this chapter, a section on effective negotiation will discuss this technique in more detail.

Even composers with set formulas for determining rates occasionally approach rates on a sliding scale. Smith notes that his pricing can be "wildly elastic" per project, "depending on how busy I am and how much I want to do it." If you are feeling uncertain about using any of these pricing structures, deciding which is best for you, or setting appropriate rates, ask your friends, mentors, and colleagues using the discussion strategies mentioned previously.

An additional factor to consider in pricing a commissioned work is the cost of traveling to attend the premiere. Will the commissioning ensemble pay for your transportation, lodging, and/or meals? If so, will they be booking your transportation and lodging or will they be reimbursing you after the premiere? In some cases, a commissioner will pay a slightly higher fee in exchange for you booking all of your travel, lodging, and meals yourself. Other ensembles may be unwilling to cover these costs. You may value a commission differently if these costs are being provided for you, or you may view them as a necessary part of the commission negotiation. Either way, it is helpful to consider the cost of attending a premiere, and many ensembles will expect to cover these costs for you.

Pricing Multimedia Projects

Video Game Scores

Video game composers are usually hired with a rate per minute of music, explains Isaac Io Schankler. The fee for composing ten minutes of music would be ten times that per-minute rate; the fee for an hour of music would be sixty times that rate. "Sometimes that rate can vary depending on the complexity of the music or the arrangement, or if you need a budget to hire musicians out of that," Schankler says. They recommend reviewing the public pay rates surveyed by GameSoundCon: "That's good to get a general feeling of what people are charging and what to ask for, both in terms of minimum rates" and in terms of experience or name recognition. (See the Resources section for a link to the survey data and pricing that Schankler cites.)

Indie video game publishers may offer composers a smaller fee alongside the opportunity to retain the rights to your work, whereas major publishers will usually offer a work-for-hire contract, which requires signing away your copyright for your music. Chapter 10 will discuss the potential pitfalls of work-for-hire contracts in greater detail.

Pricing Film Scores

Film composers are usually paid in composer fees or package deals. A package deal is a lump sum from which the composer pays themself, their musicians, and all associated recording costs. In other words, a package deal requires that the composer plan out the cost of producing their film score and then budget accordingly. By contrast, with a composer fee, "the studio pays for the production cost, the recording, the copying, the orchestration, the mixing, all of that stuff, and then you get your fee," Dara Taylor says. She very much prefers for a studio to pay her fee separately, then cover the recording and production costs. That way, she doesn't have to worry about making her own budget or having to hire musicians for reduced rates; she just focuses on writing the music. Even when the studio is paying for production costs, though, Taylor must keep the studio's budget in mind. Payments from film studios often arrives in thirds: one third is paid after a composer begins working on the music, another third before recording starts, and the final third when the music has been delivered and the project is complete. While a package deal may be preferable to a composer fee, the former is unfortunately much more common than the latter. For that reason, film composers must learn to antici-pate their budget when they take on a project with a package deal.

"Sometimes in negotiation for whatever that package fee is going to be," Taylor says, "we have to discuss, 'Okay, what's the instrumentation? How much do we need to pay for?'" She also ensures that hiring and recording vocalists is not covered in her package deal, especially if those singers will need to be affil-iated with a union, such as the Screen Actors Guild (SAG-AFTRA). "When it's a package deal, there's a lot more complication when it comes to negotiation and contracts."

Jeff Beal notes that film composers may have little room for negotiation in pricing. "Nine times out of ten, long before a composer is hired, the film budget is set," he says. "I have a really great agent, and she knows when she can push" for a higher fee, but "it's very rare." More often, with a bigger studio, Beal notes, "the fee is the fee. If you really want to do it, you say yes." With smaller independent films, on the other hand, there's more room for negoti-ation. "One of the important deal points will be the number of musicians on the score," Beal says. "A common number is four or five musicians for an all-in independent film package. On those small projects, I have quite a few times said [to my agent], 'Okay, just do the deal. Get me in the door; get me hired.'"

Beal notes that once he has been hired on a project and has created great mockup recordings, there may be more flexibility to hire additional musicians. "At a certain point in the meeting [with the filmmaker], I'll just look over and say, 'You know, it'd be really nice if we had an orchestra on this.'" In these conversations, Beal emphasizes to the filmmaking team that hiring additional musicians may only cost the studio another $15,000 to $20,000 in exchange for a much fuller sound. If their collaboration has gone well thus far, the studio may be open to spending extra money on additional musicians.

Both Beal and Taylor note the importance of protecting your own com-posing fee on a project paid as a package deal. While you still want to deliver a beautiful score on a small budget, Beal says, you also want to make sure you don't overspend on hiring additional musicians out of your budget, or else you'll watch your own profit "go up in smoke."

Setting Sliding-Scale Rates

Even as an established professional, you may encounter situations where your pricing necessitates flexibility. If you are creating a new piece for a friend, should you charge them less than your usual rate, or nothing at all? You may want to give them a "friend discount," especially if you know they don't have the budget to pay your standard fee. Luckily, sliding-scale rates offer a flexible solution for keeping your integrity and still feeling that your work is valued.

Schankler will sometimes adjust their video game–scoring rates based on whether they truly believe in the project and want to take it on. They also take a company's financial state into consideration. While they are unlikely to lower their rates for a big company or a known publisher, they may consider accepting a smaller fee from a low-budget independent company or student developer. Recently, they took on a new project with a student at New York University. "I didn't charge her my full rate," Schankler says of that project, "because she was a student and also because I thought the project was really cool and I wanted to be part of it."

A sliding-scale rate may also apply to concert-music commissions, depending on the size and budget of the organization commissioning you. Within the United States, you can look up a nonprofit's annual budget through GuideStar or other state and federal databases and adjust your rates accordingly. If the ensemble is a nonprofit, their tax records and annual budget will be on public record if their average gross revenue exceeds $50,000. If you cannot find public records for a nonprofit's finances, that likely means they have gross revenue under $50,000, and that may inform your rate. If an organization has a budget of $100,000 a year, you may want to quote a different rate than what you would quote for an organization with a million-dollar annual budget. You may also be able to find specific information on how much money has been allocated toward projects in the past or view a list of donors and donations on an organization's website to give you a sense of their budget. Other countries have similar database resources, such as the Charity Commission in the United Kingdom. (See the Resources section for US-based links.) A quick online search can likely yield a government-maintained database for nonprofit organizations in other countries.

Whatever you are charging for your music—or even if you are not charging anything—you and your collaborator(s) should articulate the terms of your collaboration in a written letter of agreement. An agreement between you and your commissioner doesn't have to be incredibly formal or worded in legalese to serve as a simple statement of your terms. Even when working for free or with a friend, your letter of agreement should include the length of the piece, the instrumentation, when the piece is due, and the terms of any premiere performance or recording rights.

Raising Your Rates

Maybe you have a set rate that you've been charging, but you are starting to feel that you have outgrown it. Or maybe you learn that a colleague is charging a drastically higher—or lower—rate, which can throw your pricing strategy into a tailspin. When you've taken on several projects and know your work is getting stronger with that additional experience, how and when do you decide to raise your rates? How do you assess your market value, independent of what people are willing to pay you and regardless of what you've previously been charging?

It's easier to raise your rates once you've started charging money for your work, even if your initial rates are low. From there, all it takes for you to scale your rate higher is for one person to believe you are worth more than the rate you have been charging. This is one perk of asking a commissioning party about their budget first in a negotiation: they may suggest a number that is much higher than your current rate.

In Dale Trumbore's pricing, she likes to ask for a number slightly above what feels comfortable. She can tell it is time to raise her rates when she feels too comfortable with the number she is currently charging, or when she has been charging that rate for two years—whichever comes first. Many composers also raise their rates when they're receiving more requests for work than they can reasonably take on. For example, if you are charging $1,000/minute for your work and find that your work is in very high demand, you might consider raising your rate to $1,500 or even $2,000/minute.

Frank Ticheli employed this method in his own career, particularly when he began receiving numerous requests to guest-conduct his work as well as to write new compositions. He increased his rates as his schedule backed up, thinking the new, higher rates would deter some of his potential collaborators. To Ticheli's surprise, "that didn't have any effect." If anything, there seemed to be even *more* demand for his work: more offers to guest-conduct and compose new commissions. "That's interesting psychologically, isn't it?" he says. "I was trying to run people off, and instead there were more offers."

Even if you must decline some projects after raising your rates, you'll make similar or more income in exchange for doing less overall work. As in Ticheli's example, if higher pricing is prohibitive for a few collaborators, the demand for your work still suggests you will work steadily. You can also consider offering a consortium at a lower cost to all co-commissioners, a strategy discussed later in this chapter.

Weighing Publishing, Self-Publishing, and Distribution

When Eric Whitacre began his professional career in the early 1990s, there was a perception that "you weren't a composer until you were published." This led to Whitacre making business deals and signing contracts that he never would have signed had he known the full legal ramifications of giving up his copyright. Ultimately, he says, being published had "relatively small importance" in his career, and he took issue with how his published works were engraved and marketed.

"It just all seemed so old-fashioned and static," he says, "and I thought, *There's this whole other way to be doing this.* I decided to publish *A Boy and a Girl*, which I wrote in 2002, under my own imprint." At that time, Whitacre had already been self-publishing his concert band pieces for several years. He found that managing his own pieces made them flourish, with greater sales results than he was finding with his published work. He attempted to buy back his published catalog, but the publisher refused to sell them. Attempting to buy back his catalog was never about making more money, Whitacre says. Rather, his desire to buy back his catalog was motivated by wanting the best for his music, which he views as an extension of himself.

As Whitacre notes, publishing a piece with a traditional publishing house used to be regarded as the gold standard for composers. Publishing houses served as a supposed arbiter of quality, making it easy for conductors and soloists to select from curated repertoire. While the ability to distribute music through the internet has drastically disrupted that model, there are still several advantages to publishing your work. Publishers may provide insightful editing comments as they prepare to engrave your work. They may provide free demo recording services, generating a high-quality recording of your work and/or selling practice tracks of your music. They may also promote your music in a variety of ways: on social media, via email, in physical catalogs, at conference booths, and at conference reading sessions. For composers who do not wish to print physical copies, publishers can provide that service in the form of printing scores on demand or storing them in a warehouse.

There is one big downside to publishing your work, however: publishing your work with a traditional publishing house almost always means signing over your copyright. When you give away your copyright, you lose the right to decide who licenses or arranges that music. Traditional music publishing offers a royalty rate of only 10–20 percent, and that rate is further divided if you set a text by a living author to music. Under this traditional model, your royalty rate with a traditional publisher could be as low as 5 percent. Publishers can also take a piece out of print if they decide it isn't selling enough copies, though this practice is less common with digital and print-on-demand scores. They can also deny you the right to arrange your own music.

Dale Trumbore once asked her publisher whether she could arrange *I Am Music*, a piece she had originally written for SATB chorus and piano, to be performed by a TTBB choir. Her editor responded that at this time, he'd "have to pass" on the new voicing, since the SATB version had not sold well enough to merit another arrangement. Trumbore was offered a one-time license to create a TTBB version for a single performance, after which the new arrangement would not be published, nor would Trumbore be permitted to self-publish or distribute it on her own. This experience—being denied the chance to arrange and sell her own music—soured Trumbore on traditional publishing, and she has vowed to never give up her copyright again.

By contrast, self-publishing your work allows you to keep your copyright and your profit. You are also solely responsible for engraving and promoting that music, handling sales, and managing physical and/or digital distribution. Some composers delegate the various tasks involved in self-publishing by hiring an assistant to help with score sales. Others sell PDFs through their website, automatically watermarking those digital scores with help from website plugins.

Alex Shapiro has been self-publishing her works for decades, a decision she made early in her career that has served her well. "I always knew I would self-publish because I'm a control freak and want to maintain all the control over everything," she says. "You're never going to have more incentive to run your business well and to understand the worth of what you're selling and your intellectual property, than when you are publishing your own catalog." The biggest classical music publishers, like Boosey & Hawkes or G. Schirmer, have traditionally offered promotional services. But as Shapiro notes, even if you were to sign with a major publisher, "No one is going to represent you better than you." While a publisher will handle engraving, order fulfillment, and some promotion of your works, "you're still going to have to show up and be out there in the world to let people know that this music exists."

Still, Shapiro notes, "some publishers are really great and can be very helpful to composers, plenty of whom are not the kind of people who want to be running their own business." Composers with full-time day jobs, including teaching or other nine-to-five positions, may prefer to publish their works traditionally. In doing so, they intentionally give away their copyright and accept a low royalty rate in exchange for not having to handle any of the administrative work that accompanies self-publishing. The amount of work that self-publishing requires can admittedly be daunting, as it can involve managing not only score sales but also licensing your works.

In recent years, a third option has arrived to disrupt the publishing versus self-publishing models: distributors. (See Table 6.1 for a comparison of publishers, distributors, and self-publishing.) Distributors offer a market-place in which composers can sell their work in exchange for a larger royalty percentage than that offered by publishers. Unlike a publisher, a distributor will not take your copyright. Music distributors may offer anywhere between 25–75 percent of net sales royalties to a composer—a stark contrast to the standard 10–20 percent offered by traditional publishers. Many composers find working with a distributor to be an ideal balance of the trade-offs between traditional publishing and self-publishing, with few downsides. (For examples of music distributors, see the Resources section.)

There is an inherent paradox in the decision of whether or not to publish traditionally. When you are starting your career and could most benefit from the promotion that a publisher would provide, publishers may be unwilling to publish you, as you are largely unknown. When you are already established in your career, though—when you no longer need the boost in attention that a traditional publisher can provide—a publisher is more likely to want to represent you.

This dynamic has played out in Mari Esabel Valverde's career, as one of Valverde's compositions was initially rejected by several publishers. It wasn't until years later, after the piece had been commercially recorded by an ensemble overseas and broadcast on American radio, that some of the same people who had rejected the piece finally expressed interest in performing or

Table 6.1 Different Publishing Models for Composers

	Publishers	Distributors	Self-Publishing
Does the composer keep copyright?	No	Yes	Yes
Average royalty rate offered	5–20%	25–75%	Up to 100%, minus administrative costs
Advantages	Showcases and, in some cases, promotes your music. Engraves and sells music.	May promote your music. Composer retains all rights.	Great rate of profit, especially with a "hit piece." Composer retains all rights.
Disadvantages	May introduce errors when engraving your music. Composer loses all rights to their music.	Composer's music may not be promoted if the distributor has a large catalog.	Composer is solely responsible for the work of engraving, promoting, and selling.

publishing it. "It took them a decade of other folks believing in and investing in me to decide my work was worthy of their interest," she says.

For Valverde, the decision of whether to self-publish or publish traditionally hasn't been an easy one. Valverde deeply regrets her decision to publish one of her pieces traditionally, noting that "the engraving is awful; it's microscopic." This is a common experience for many composers: in the process of engraving your music into their notation system, traditional publishers often introduce errors and strange formatting choices into your music, and it is often your job—not your editor's—to catch those errors in early proofs. Valverde hopes to someday buy back from the publisher the rights to that piece. Still, the decision to publish another piece traditionally early on in her career led to some of Valverde's initial successes as a choral composer. Many composers decide to publish a few pieces traditionally at the start of their careers, if that option is available to them, and then self-publish the rest of their catalog, with or without a distributor. This strategy may be particularly relevant to choral composers. As with many financial decisions, only you can decide what is right for your career.

Pricing Your Scores

If you decide to self-publish some or all of your work, you'll be the one pricing your scores. Some distributors also allow composers to set their own prices. To determine what you should be charging, you'll want to first see what your competitors—composers with pieces of a similar length, difficulty level, and instrumentation—are charging for their works.

"You can see pricing structures for a lot of things online," Juhi Bansal says. "It's not hard to get a sense of what other people are charging or what groups are paying." Let's say you are trying to price an eight-minute work for Grade 3 wind ensemble. You could research what pieces of a similar length and scope cost when they are sold by traditional publishers, distributors, and self-published composers. From there, you could average those prices and use that average to price your own score and parts.

Derrick Skye prices his scores affordably so that most ensembles will be able to access his music and potentially form a longer, lasting relationship with him and his music. For Skye, the objective "isn't really to sell a bunch of copies, or to get a bunch of streams. It's to be paid to engage in projects and build relationships."

Alex Shapiro views score prices similarly to Skye, noting a hypothetical situation in which one $80 score sale could lead a conductor to hire her for a $200 online rehearsal, which—if the online rehearsal helps foster a relationship with that conductor—might ultimately lead them to co-commissioning her through a consortium. "That's upselling in the nicest of ways," she says. "Nobody should ever look at their income stream or at their career as just some isolated thing of 'score sales here and residencies there and commissions there.' It's all interconnected because of these relationships." For Shapiro, it has been beautiful to witness these relationships with collaborators evolve. "It's never just about that piece of music they bought," she says. "It's about the friendship you're building with them and the colleagueship."

Just as commissioning rates can operate on a sliding scale, score sales can also operate under a flexible pricing structure. For example, Melissa Dunphy has a unique policy in place for score pricing: performers and conductors only need to pay for her digital sheet music if they are charging an admission fee for their concerts. If a performance is free of charge, like a student recital or a church service, concert presenters can download and print her sheet music for free, so long as they notify Dunphy and her team about concert details and send a concert program after the performance. Several of her scores are also available under a flexible "name your price" model. "It makes absolutely no sense for me to put any kind of barrier on access to my scores," Dunphy says. "The more people get my scores, the more people are exposed to my music, the more performances I will get, and the more commissions I will get."

While Dunphy's model is somewhat uncommon, it showcases her commitment to valuing long-term relationship building over the shorter goal of immediate monetary gain. This approach also maximizes Dunphy's audience, which in turn increases opportunities for future commissions. In other words, rather than prioritizing the short-term gain of score sales, a flexible score pricing model prioritizes the long-term goal of securing commissions, which generally offer a much larger monetary gain.

If you self-publish your music, you can also keep a database of the individuals who purchase your music: their name, their affiliated ensemble (if any), and their physical and/or email address. This information can be useful when you are putting together a mailing list, touring or otherwise traveling for work, or publishing a new composition that may appeal to those who have purchased a similar piece in the past. Some music distributors also track individual score purchase orders and pass along this information, but publishing houses traditionally do not share this information with composers.

Organizing Consortiums

What should you do when a potential collaborator wants to commission you, but they offer a number that feels too low? What if you have a piece in mind that you would love to write but no collaborator to help bring your goal to fruition? A consortium is often the solution to either problem, bridging the gap between your desire to bring a piece to life and your need to make money writing it. If a collaborator can't afford to pay you your asking rate, you can always consider bringing additional co-commissioners into a project.

What's a Consortium?

A consortium is a group of ensembles or soloists who pool resources to jointly commission a new piece of music. Some composers we interviewed shared that they use consortiums to make artistically fulfilling or grand-scale projects happen: a new work for soprano and orchestra, for example, or a concert-length work for any ensemble. When no single ensemble or organization volunteers to commission such a substantial project, or when a commissioning fee is dauntingly steep, a consortium may be the answer.

In a two-ensemble consortium, one commissioner might pay slightly more—say, 60–80 percent of the commissioning fee—to give the world premiere of a work. The second commissioner would pay slightly less to give a regional premiere that would take place after the world premiere. The consortium model can also involve a larger number of ensembles, organizations, or solo performers splitting the cost of a new piece evenly. Sometimes these ensembles each give a regional premiere of a piece, and other times geographic location is not a factor: anyone can join the consortium.

Consortiums are also a great way to generate multiple performances of the same piece. After a standard premiere, it can be challenging to find a second performer for your new composition, but a consortium guarantees multiple performances of that work from the outset. These performances translate to more audience exposure across a broader region. Furthermore, when a composer organizes a consortium for a longer work or for many performances of the new piece, performance royalties have the potential to generate significant additional income beyond the total commissioning fee. These performance royalties may not be paid out by your performing rights organization (PRO) for up to twenty-three months after the performance, but that potential additional income should still be taken into account when a composer is weighing the benefits of a consortium. (Chapter 7 will discuss PROs and performance royalties in greater detail.)

Examples of Successful Consortiums

In 2015, Timothy C. Takach organized a consortium for his piece *The Longest Nights*, a seven-movement choral cycle accessible to high schools, collegiate choirs, and community ensembles. Takach had the idea to find fifty co-commissioners to make the overall commissioning cost accessible:

> I wanted to find one choir from every state [in the United States] to help bring this thing to life. It also helped with the idea that they would be the premiering choir from Rhode Island, or they would have the Vermont premiere, or California, wherever they were. . . . So it made it easier to define who I was looking for, and it also was easier for me to check boxes and say, "I already have New Jersey. I don't need to look for New Jersey anymore. What's next? Where else should I go? And what states am I not known in?" . . . It was a challenge to find all those groups. I think I ended up with forty-two total, so I didn't hit my mark. But it was enough for me to say, "This is worth my time. I got paid a good fee for this, and it's getting performed forty-two times across the United States."

Takach's goal of reaching out to new choirs to expand his network across the country served him well, and he is using the same approach for another consortium.

Dale Trumbore has organized several consortiums of ten to fifteen co-commissioners who each paid $250–500 for the regional premiere rights to a new composition. She has also participated in consortiums with two to five co-commissioners, where a lead ensemble pays $1,000–5,000 for the premiere rights to a piece and additional co-commissioners pay between $750 and $2,000. Because of the success of those past collaborations, Trumbore now mentions the possibility of putting together a consortium in nearly every initial conversation with a potential collaborator. She uses the following script, which you are welcome to adapt or borrow: "My usual rate is [this much money], but if that rate feels out of range, I'd be happy to discuss putting together a consortium with one or more co-commissioners."

Different Consortium Models

Here are several different models for consortiums, some of which are similar to the examples above:

Model 1

All commissioners pay the same amount of money to commission a new work.

- Commissioners may give a regional premiere of the work or may have a set window of time (e.g., a year) in which to give their performance, with no regional restrictions for participation in the consortium.
- Example: Fifteen high school jazz bands from across the United States co-commission a new ten-minute work. Each one pays $1,000, so the composer makes $15,000. Over the course of a year, the piece receives fifteen performances across the United States.

Model 2

One lead commissioner pays more for the right to give the world premiere of a new composition. One or more co-commissioners pay a smaller amount to give regional premieres of the work.

- This could take the form of a co-commission—two commissioners involved—or three or more commissioners.
- Regional restrictions for participation in the consortium could take the form of one ensemble per state, as in Takach's consortium; one ensemble per region; one ensemble per country; or some combination of the above.
- Example: One soprano pays $500 for the world premiere rights to a new song cycle, and four other sopranos co-commission the piece for $250 each. The composer makes $1,500. Between the five sopranos, the piece receives a world premiere in Texas; a Southwest premiere in Arizona; a Midwest premiere in Minnesota; a Northeast premiere in New Hampshire; and a Canadian premiere in Quebec.

> ## Model 3
>
> One lead commissioner pays for the right to give the world premiere of a new work. One or more co-commissioners pay an equal or smaller amount to give the premieres of a different instrumentation of this new work.
>
> - This kind of consortium requires more work from the composer, as it necessitates creating two or more arrangements of the same piece.
> - Example: A string quartet and a string orchestra co-commission a new ten-minute work for $3,000 and $5,000, respectively. The composer makes $8,000. The composer writes the string quartet version of the piece first, then arranges the work for string orchestra. The piece receives premieres in two locations (e.g., Mexico City and Los Angeles).

Planning a Consortium

To put together your own consortium you must be a project manager in ways that are not required for regular commissions. You'll want to leave plenty of time to plan, launch, and execute the consortium. Before you officially launch a consortium, identify potential partners and be ready to approach them with a well-designed proposal that outlines the project's scope, commissioning tiers, budget, timeline, and benefits.

While putting together a consortium yourself means relying on your personal network, you can also enlist the help of that network in recruiting co-commissioners. For example, when a conductor joins your consortium, you might ask if they can recommend any other conductors whom you should also approach about joining. You will likely want to share the consortium details in relevant social media groups or other sites relevant to the community you're targeting. If your commission involves one lead commissioner, they may also be prepared to help with the majority of recruiting for the project, reaching out to their own network and sharing within that community.

When you calculate your timeline for a consortium, factor in however much time you'll need to compose the piece before delivering it to the participating ensembles. In the timeline, consider including an exclusivity period (e.g., six months or a year) in which only the commissioning ensembles have the right to perform the piece. This is often appealing to consortium members: they will be the only ones to perform this work for a set amount of time. In addition, consider leaving at least three months between the launch of your consortium and the deadline to participate, so that prospective commissioners can contemplate joining the consortium with ample time to program the piece, budget, and fundraise as needed.

Questions for Consortium Planning

A consortium requires a great deal of administrative work and planning. You'll need to create multiple letters of agreement for your project and consider several additional factors. Here are questions to ask yourself:

- Will one ensemble serve as lead commissioner on this project, receiving the world premiere of the work and paying more for that privilege, or will participants buy in equally?
- If there is a lead commissioner, will you enlist their help in recruiting consortium members, or will you rely instead on your personal network?
- If there is no lead commissioner for this consortium, will you restrict participating ensembles by region (or state) or will you allow any interested ensemble to join, regardless of region?
- What is the deadline for participants to sign up for the consortium?
- What is your deadline for delivering full scores (and parts, if applicable) to the participants?
- What is the exclusivity period for each commissioner to perform the piece?
- If there is a lead commissioner, does the ensemble have a period of exclusivity in which to give the world premiere, after which an additional period of exclusivity allows the co-commissioner(s) to give regional premieres?
- Does the lead commissioner or any other ensemble retain first refusal rights to make a commercial recording of your work?
- Are you attending any of the consortium rehearsals and performances in person? If yes, which ensemble(s) are paying for your travel expenses?

Forming a consortium may sound daunting, and it certainly requires a lot of advance planning. But as discussed above, a consortium allows you a great deal of freedom over what music you are writing, when you will deliver it, and how much you would like to be paid. Some composers use commissions as a practical financial tool: when you have a lull or lapse in commissions, you can fill the gap in your schedule with a self-initiated consortium. Other composers may join forces, launching a project wherein two or more composers each write a new piece as part of a single consortium.

Whether or not you plan to organize a consortium, it is worth familiarizing yourself with this commissioning model. Ensembles sometimes form their own consortiums, uniting to approach a composer about a co-commission. Some national organizations also host recurring consortiums for their members, commissioning a different composer each year.

Deciding Whether to Accept or Decline Paid Work

Organizing a consortium puts you in charge of who is commissioning you and what music you will compose. In standard commissions, though, there are numerous factors—monetary or not—that influence whether you should say yes to a project. While you can simply trust your gut-reaction "yes" or "no," you may also find this process is less clear-cut than it initially appears. For example, an ensemble could have a tiny budget, but the project they are proposing is highly compelling, and you would have an opportunity to make royalties from it in the future. Maybe your dream collaborator is calling, but the particular project they're proposing has you underwhelmed. Perhaps you are eager to take on more paid composing work, and so your instinct is to say yes to any well-paying composing gig, no matter how demanding or dull the project may be. These factors can be confusing, and in many of these examples, there's no single right answer to whether you should say yes or no. Luckily, though, a number of the composers interviewed here recommended helpful frameworks to guide your decision.

Three Pots and People, Project, Pay

Abbie Betinis makes career decisions based on a "three pots" approach: money, relationships, and artistic development. "I guess I'm always considering money as just a piece of the value of work," she says. Each of these "pots" has a different value proposition. While money is considered a short-term gain, relationship building and artistic development can offer short, medium, and long-term rewards. As discussed in Chapter 4, it is important for artists to weigh non-monetary value alongside monetary value. Two of the "pots" Betinis mentions—relationship-building and artistic growth—are a form of non-monetary value.

Molly Joyce has a similar way of weighing whether a project is worthwhile with what she calls the "three Ps": project, people, and pay, a concept she first heard at Sō Percussion's summer institute. For both Betinis and Joyce, a project that has two out of three strong elements is usually worth taking on, even if it lacks or is weak in the third element. "Some stuff I was taking on would be [a] really cool project; great people; no pay," Joyce says. "Sometimes the pay is really good; the project's awesome; the people are lacking."

Both the "three pots" and the "three Ps" approach have a multivariable decision-making framework that can shift over time as artistic aspirations, relationships, and financial needs change. Each of these is a form of a cost-benefit analysis (CBA). CBAs are powerful tools that can help improve your decision-making about pricing and the projects you take on. There are many different ways to analyze a project, depending on the variables that are important to you.

Cost-Benefit Analysis

Cost-benefit analysis involves weighing the costs, both tangible and intangible, against the benefits of a particular opportunity. Tangible costs might include the time and resources invested in a project, while intangible costs could be related to the emotional or artistic toll it takes. On the other side of the scale, tangible benefits could be financial compensation, and intangible benefits might include personal growth, artistic development, career advancement, or other valuable connections.

Take time to carefully consider what matters most to you and what you value in your career. For some composers, immediate financial gain is crucial, while others might prioritize long-term relationships and artistic fulfillment. By creating a CBA, you can assess the true value of each opportunity and make choices that align with your goals and aspirations.

When to Turn Down Work

Thomas Kotcheff notes the importance of saying "yes" in his career, observing that "not much happened by saying no." The most exciting opportunities in a composer's career arrive after saying "yes" to an opportunity, which can make it challenging to decline work. Still, Kotcheff says, your mental health is your "number one priority." It may be hard to decline paid work, but sometimes your own well-being demands it—even if your "no" comes at the expense of a missed opportunity.

In the "people, project, pay" or "money, relationships, and artistic development" frameworks, a project that fulfills all three factors is a clear yes. Conversely, if a project has only one strong element and two weak ones, it is likely a no. Remember that you have the right to be discerning; your work has value and worth. You have the right to turn down any project that doesn't feel like the right fit. While you may include a reason for declining (e.g., citing a scheduling conflict), you are not obligated to specify a reason for declining.

Here are a few phrases you could use when declining work, particularly when you are unwilling to cite a specific reason.

- "Thanks so much for considering me for this project, but I need to politely decline."
- "I'm honored you would consider me for this commission, but I am unavailable to participate at this time."
- "While I am not the right fit for this project, I wish you good luck in moving forward with another composer. Thank you again for reaching out."

As mentioned earlier, when you decline a project, you could also consider referring one or more composer peers who *would* be an excellent fit, using a variation on the above: "While I have to decline, I'd be happy to put you in touch with [name one or more colleagues here], who I think could be a great fit for this project."

You may decide to take on a commission for any number of reasons, and those may or may not be linked to money. What you are actually considering is value: the value you gain by taking on a commission, and the value you offer to your collaborators. "How are you appraising the value of something that's not monetary?" Derrick Skye asks. He always considers the long game: how one successful collaboration with one person can unlock multiple opportunities or projects. In other words, when deciding whether or not to take on a project, he appraises *value* rather than *currency*. For Isaac Io Schankler, a worthwhile job must also include a "spark of excitement or joy." "You know we're not doing data entry, right?" Schankler says. "We're doing music." It's easy to downplay the importance of joy in our work, but it's "the core of what we do. I think you ignore that at your peril."

When you navigate the intricacies of pricing your music, your inner sense of self-worth meets significant economic considerations. Each pricing decision reflects both your current needs and your long-term vision, balancing monetary and value-driven choices with the value you bring to the world through your art. Remember that your worth as a composer extends beyond numbers: it is found in the art you create, the connections you forge, and the lasting legacy of your music.

Pricing is just one piece of the puzzle. To build a sustainable career, it is essential to diversify the ways you earn a living as a music creator. The next chapter explores how to develop a portfolio of income streams that align with your strengths. Ultimately, growing your income through passive and active sources can ensure greater financial stability, offering you more time to focus on your craft.

7

Diversifying Income Streams

As you plan for a sustainable composing career, you'll need to create multiple income streams. This may seem impossible at first, but you might view it as laying one brick at a time. This strategy may not feel like it is doing much for you financially *now*, but over time, you'll look back and realize you've created a viable path for yourself.

There are already many great books on financial literacy, so this book will not try to duplicate that advice. (See the Resources section for further reading recommendations.) Rather, this chapter will list the most common income streams for composers and explore how you can combine them into a reliable source of funding for your art. First, it is important to define a few key terms: active income, passive income, and wealth.

Understanding the Difference between Income Types and Wealth

Active Income

Active income requires your ongoing time, effort, and direct involvement. There are tools to automate some of this work, which Chapter 8 will address, but at the end of the day, active income requires your most valuable currency: time. Two examples of active income for composers are commissions and speaking gigs; later in this chapter, you'll find many more examples of active income.

Passive Income

Passive income requires minimal to no time or effort once an initial work, system, or process is completed. This is the ideal type of income because it does not require continuous time, effort, or direct involvement. Two examples of passive income for composers are royalties and score sales.

Composing a Living. Brandon Elliott and Dale Trumbore, Oxford University Press.
© Brandon Elliott and Dale Trumbore 2025. DOI: 10.1093/9780197803509.003.0008

Wealth

Wealth is a measurement of your total net worth. It is important to grasp the difference between wealth and income. Wealth adds up all of your financial assets (holdings like investments, property, or valuable objects) and then deducts any liabilities (financial obligations like credit card debt, student loan debt, or a mortgage). Because wealth can grow over long periods of time, it will help you establish ongoing financial stability and contemplate a freelance career.

To further expand on the difference between wealth and income, let's imagine a mid-career composer named Shannon. Shannon currently earns an annual income of $90,000 from various sources including college teaching, performing, and commissions. That $90,000 represents Shannon's *active income*. She also makes an additional $10,000 in *passive income*, including performance royalties, score sales, and licensing her music. Her current overall income per year is $100,000.

Over more than a decade of composing, teaching, and performing, Shannon has saved money: she has invested in stocks, funded a retirement account, purchased an apartment with a mortgage, and bought a grand piano. The total value of her property, savings, investments, and assets is $550,000. Shannon also has $250,000 in mortgage debt, $40,000 of student loan debt, and $10,000 of credit card debt. After subtracting her liabilities from her assets ($550,000 minus $300,000), her net worth is $250,000. This $250,000 represents Shannon's *wealth*.

Wealth is a measure of financial health and stability, reflecting the resources available to an individual or entity beyond their regular income. To recap: while your income refers to money you receive regularly, wealth represents your total accumulation of assets minus liabilities. While it would be impossible to list every way composers earn money, here are the most common active and passive income streams that composers rely on to establish a regular income and lay the groundwork—brick by brick—toward building wealth.

Examples of Active Income

Commissions and Other Composing Gigs

Most composers make the bulk of their active income from composing original works for ensembles, soloists, companies, or other organizations.

This can include everything from chamber music and large-ensemble works to work-for-hire projects like film and video-game scores. Commissions usually provide a significant portion of a composer's income. Your commissioning fee can and should increase over time as you garner experience.

Speaking Gigs

Speaking gigs may include participating in conferences, guest lectures, seminars, and workshops. Sharing your expertise and experiences can be both rewarding and lucrative. These engagements can enhance your reputation and provide networking opportunities. For composers, speaking gigs take a variety of forms, which may include giving a pre-concert talk; sitting in on a rehearsal (in person or virtually) to provide feedback; hosting a clinic, workshop, or master class; or spending several days in residence with students, which may include a combination of the above gigs along with guest teaching one or more classes. When you are invited for a speaking gig, always ask what the budget is for the engagement.

Teaching

Composition teaching gigs may include giving private lessons, conducting master classes, or teaching at educational institutions. Teaching not only supplements income but also helps in building a community and mentoring the next generation of musicians. As noted in Chapter 2, seeing others succeed and knowing that you played a small role in their success can provide a sense of personal and professional fulfillment. Teaching and mentorship fill this role in many composers' lives.

Performing or Conducting

Many composers also perform or conduct their own music or music by others in concerts, recitals, and recordings. Conducting, performing, and other forms of musical collaboration can generate income and increase your visibility in the music community. Composers like Zanaida Stewart Robles and Frank Ticheli have developed careers as both composers and conductors, while others, like Angélica Negrón and Shara Nova, notably perform their own music. If you are a composer-conductor, you may be invited to workshop or guest-conduct your own work in performance. Similarly, you may be invited to give a concert of your work where you are expected to both perform and workshop your compositions with other musicians. Make sure you feel your time is being adequately compensated. For example, if you wrote a piece for piano and string quartet and you are invited to perform the piano part, you would ideally receive payment for this engagement beyond your commission fee.

Side Gigs

Developing side skills, musical or not, can provide additional income streams. Based on the composer interviews for this book, here are some examples of side gigs:

Arranger/Orchestrator
Arrangers and orchestrators may work alone or with a collaborator (e.g., arranging for a traditional publishing house or orchestrating for a film composer). Arranging or orchestrating music can provide active income, but these jobs can also provide additional passive income in the form of royalties.

Assistant
Assistants provide support for other composers. As we'll discuss in the following chapter, many composers reach a point where they need assistance with career management: help with invoicing, score sales, website maintenance, social media presence, or the score-editing work mentioned above. Working as an assistant for another composer could help you gain valuable experience that may ultimately inform how you structure your own composing career.

Grant Writer
Grant writers help organizations secure funding. If you have strong writing, communication, and research skills, this skill can be valuable in securing grants for your projects or for other ensembles with whom you are collaborating.

Engraver/Copyist
Engravers and copyists improve notation and provide score-editing services for traditional publishers or other composers. Established composers and

those who compose by ear often hire other composers for engraving jobs that could include transcription work, parts preparation, or copyediting. If you are meticulous about the presentation of your own scores, you may be interested in engraving or copyist work.

Recording Engineer

As a recording engineer, you could offer recording services for other musicians or engineer your own recordings. Working as a recording engineer can build upon your existing composing skills, especially if you already have a home studio or are used to working within a DAW.

Website Developer

Web developers create and manage websites for musicians and other clients. A strong online presence is crucial in today's digital age, and this skill is always in high demand.

Diversifying Your Active Income

The more diversified your skill set is, the more diverse your active income streams will be. There's no set formula for combining passive and active income to guarantee a "successful" composing career. Rather, a career as a composer allows for many possible income pathways. Remember: *There's no single right way to make a living writing music.*

If your career isn't flowing in the direction you would like, Juhi Bansal recommends trying to view it as if it were someone else's business, asking, "What else is there that you can maximize and turn into an income stream or develop into an income stream?" As you contemplate ways to diversify your own active income, consider the following questions:

- What skills beyond composing do you already possess?
- What "side gig" skills could you potentially monetize?
- Are there new skills adjacent to your existing expertise that you could either learn or strengthen?

Keep in mind that the earlier list of ways to generate active income is not exhaustive; you may have other, better ideas for how to supplement and diversify your composing income. Your answer may also involve work that is completely unrelated to the music field.

Examples of Passive Income

While active income streams are a great way to build wealth, passive income streams are even more desirable as you establish your career. These can feel like "free money": checks and direct deposits that simply arrive in your mailbox or inbox, with little to no additional effort required on your part. These opportunities include royalty streams and licensing placements.

"The various forms of licensing are dictated by a murky swamp of laws that lag behind advances in technology and distribution," Jake Runestad says, and it can certainly be confusing to consider the many different ways to license your music. This section will clarify the various kinds of licensing and other ways to generate passive income, starting with a few of the most common types of passive income streams.

Sales Royalties

Sales royalties are the income you generate from selling your sheet music through various platforms, depending on whether you choose to publish traditionally, self-publish, or sell your music through a marketplace (or a combination of all the above). Each sale generates royalties, providing a steady—albeit unpredictable—stream of income.

Performance Royalties

Performance royalties are your earnings from performances of your compositions. These are collected by performing rights organizations (PROs) when your music is played live or broadcast. You can also choose to execute a direct license for performances if you would rather not deal with a third-party PRO. As previously discussed, PRO payments for a performance of your work may not arrive until up to twenty-three months after that performance has occurred. Refer to the section "Navigating PROs or Direct Licensing" later in this chapter for more information about performing royalties and PROs.

Mechanical Licensing

This form of income comes from licensing the rights to reproduce and distribute your music. When your compositions are recorded and sold (physically or digitally), mechanical royalties are generated. In the United States, rates determined by the government are used to calculate these royalties. You can find the current rates, set per track or per minute of recorded playing time, by looking up the "Statutory Mechanical Royalty Rate."

If you publish your music traditionally, your publisher will likely execute and oversee mechanical licensing agreements and send you a portion of the royalties based on your particular publishing agreement. If you self-publish or sell through a marketplace as a self-publisher, you'll individually execute your own mechanical license and collect 100 percent of the royalties.

Synchronization (or "Sync") Licensing

Sync licensing is the use of your music in visual media such as films, TV shows, video games, social media, and more. It can be a significant income source, especially if your music is used in high-profile projects. While mechanical royalty rates are established by the Copyright Royalty Board (CRB), there is no set contract or template to use to negotiate synchronization royalties. Consider reaching out to peers, colleagues, and mentors to ask if you can view or adapt their template for such a contract. Sync licensing rates are negotiated between the owner of a musical recording and the user of that musical recording. Generally, the more popular and in demand your music is, the more you can charge for a sync license.

When you set your sync licensing rate, consider factors like the nature and type of usage for your music. For example, if a student-run string quartet wants to post a video performing your piece, you may choose to charge little to nothing in synchronization fees. If a professional organization wants to post a video of a live performance of your music, you might charge them more than you would a low-budget community ensemble. Some composers may have a zero-tolerance policy for the unlicensed posting of their works (without a sync license) and may request to have these videos taken down or require that the video owner pay a synchronization fee. Other composers may allow even unlicensed videos to remain, as these videos could allow their music to be more easily discovered. As with many aspects of a career in music, there is no single "right answer" to how much you should be charging for a sync license.

Placement for Film/TV/Videos

Placement is a branch of synchronization licensing. Placing your music in visual media often requires networking and working with music supervisors. The income from sync placements can vary but often includes an upfront fee plus royalties. Getting just a few placements can be extremely lucrative both upon execution of the contract and for several years, or sometimes until perpetuity.

Recordings

Recordings include physical copies of your music (e.g., CDs or vinyl) and digital downloads. These can provide notable income. Additionally, streaming platforms like Spotify and Apple Music generate royalties based on the number of plays. While the per-play rate is incredibly low, cumulative plays could add up over time to another passive income stream for your most popular tracks.

Digital Performance Royalties

Distinctly different from mechanical royalties, digital performance royalties are collected by organizations like SoundExchange when your music is streamed on non-interactive platforms such as satellite radio. Unlike traditional performance royalties, digital performance royalties are split between the performer and the copyright holder.

Neighboring Rights

These rights address the public performances of recorded tracks. However, as a composer and presumptive copyright holder of the music, you are only owed neighboring rights if you are also a performer or producer of the recording. In the United States, neighboring rights are less developed than in other countries, but they still represent an additional revenue stream, especially for composers whose works are played internationally. Collective rights management organizations can help gather any additional royalties owed to you.

Copyright, Publishing, and Royalties

"It's the responsibility of an artist to understand there are potential investments in their copyright," Abbie Betinis says, noting that holding onto a copyright can generate a return on investment in the form of multiple passive income streams. "Understand how copyright works so that you are making money on the mechanical and sync licensing, publishing, distribution, reprints, and performances, not just holding on to the copyright for dear life." The potential passive income streams listed in the previous section yield the greatest potential for income generation if you are the copyright holder for the music being licensed. When you give up your copyright in order to publish a work, though, your publisher then assumes responsibility for licensing your work and collecting mechanical and/or sync royalties related to that licensing. These royalties will traditionally be split equally between you and the publisher.

Even given the financial and artistic advantages to keeping your copyright, some composers—particularly those with a full-time job outside of composition—view the publisher royalty split and subsequent loss of income favorably. These composers may prefer to have a publisher manage their licensing income because they value their time—specifically, the time they don't have to spend processing licensing requests—more than the potential income generated from licensing royalties.

Navigating PROs or Direct Licensing

Performing rights organizations (PROs) are responsible for collecting and distributing performance royalties. Melissa Dunphy recognizes that while commissions are indeed the largest portion of her income pie chart, performance royalties are the second largest. "Performance royalties [are] pretty big money, especially if you self-publish," she says.

Most composers choose to join a PRO, although you can also choose to direct-license a performance of your work whether or not you have joined one. PROs are governed by a combination of consent decrees, statutes, Title 17 of the United States Code, and the Copyright Royalty Board (CRB). Many countries have their own PRO(s) to collect and distribute performance royalties to composers. In the United States, the main PROs are ASCAP, BMI, and SESAC. Each has its unique features and advantages.

While it's possible to switch from one PRO to another, you can only belong to one PRO covering a given territory at any time. Limited-territory agreements are also possible; these agreements are concurrent, but cover unique territories. Most composers are members of just one PRO at any given time. Each PRO boasts proprietary algorithms and data collection methods to track performances, though these methods may not capture most classical concert performances. The exact formulas for calculating royalty payouts for each PRO are closely guarded.

There's one aspect of joining a PRO that's rarely talked about, particularly in classical concert music, which can provide a substantial benefit over direct licensing: non-recoupable advances. A non-recoupable royalty advance is a fixed annual amount that you receive every year, regardless of the performance history that year. Your PRO may offer you a non-recoupable advance once your annual royalties reach higher amounts. For classical concert music composers, these amounts might start at a few thousand dollars annually and increase to a substantial five- or six-figure amount. While there is public information available about the existence of these non-recoupable advances, there is none available on how these advances are calculated or who is eligible to receive them. Composers who are approached about a non-recoupable advance or successfully negotiate for one will likely be asked to sign a non-disclosure agreement.

American Society of Composers, Authors, and Publishers (ASCAP)

Owned and run by its members, ASCAP is the only US nonprofit PRO offering a straightforward registration process and extensive educational resources. If you are a composer who self-publishes, you'll need to register your works with ASCAP as both composer and publisher of your work. While it is free to join ASCAP as a composer, there is, at time of publication, a one-time $50 fee to join as a publisher.

ASCAP offers additional and robust support and resources tailored to composers, including educational workshops and networking opportunities. Some composers also enjoy affiliating with ASCAP because of their nonprofit operations, but other composers may argue that affiliating with a for-profit business like BMI might mean higher payouts. Ultimately, you will need to evaluate your own performance patterns, goals, and the specific services and support each PRO offers to determine which aligns best with your needs.

Broadcast Music, Inc. (BMI)

Known for its support of new and emerging artists, BMI provides similar services to ASCAP but is organized as a for-profit corporation. In 2024, BMI was acquired by New Mountain Capital, a growth-oriented investment firm. The stated intention of BMI's acquisition and transition to a for-profit entity is to accelerate growth, which, ultimately, benefits their members. However, the transition from a nonprofit organization to a for-profit entity—combined with an acquisition—has led to some concern and uncertainty among members. If you are a composer who self-publishes your work, you do not need to register additionally as a publisher with BMI. BMI may offer higher payouts than ASCAP in some scenarios, due to its royalty calculation methods. BMI also emphasizes detailed performance data, and its technology-driven approach can be advantageous for composers seeking transparency and efficiency in royalty distribution.

SESAC (Society of European Stage Authors and Composers)

A selective PRO that operates on an invitation-only basis, SESAC is known for its personalized service and efficiency. Because it is a for-profit organization, SESAC can often offer higher royalty rates and more personalized service, but it is also more selective in its membership.

Performance Reporting

Especially in the concert music space, PROs rely on the composer, the performing ensemble, or the presenting organization to submit a report or concert program through their performance notification system, which could be an online form to fill out or an email submission process. Note that PROs serve a much larger population of popular music artists than classical composers, and their proprietary systems don't necessarily work optimally for classical concert music.

Whether you publish traditionally or choose to self-publish, you should take responsibility for reporting your performances to your PRO. There is no harm in multiple sources (e.g., a composer and a presenting organization) reporting the same performance, but if you neglect to report a performance, you risk not being paid performance royalties for it. To keep track of performances, many composers set Google alerts for their name and the names of their compositions, while other composers set aside some time each month to search for that information and save PDFs of concert information (e.g., a concert announcement, an event listing, or a digital copy of a concert program). You may also want to save hard copies of concert programs that include your music, which you can mail in to a PRO or convert to a PDF for online submission. Note that not all concerts are eligible for PRO payouts. For example, PROs do not typically license K–12 performances, religious services, or student degree recitals. If you join a PRO, they will provide guidelines on what types of performances qualify for royalties. If you are ever unsure, always err on the side of reporting.

A performing organization can generally opt for a per-concert license, where they submit quarterly payments to PROs based on the specific concerts and repertoire they perform. At time of publication, BMI no longer offers a per-concert license. Alternatively, performing organizations can opt for a blanket license where there is an annual minimum fee that covers most performances, but they can be subject to overages based on their performance history each quarter. Both ASCAP and BMI have online portals where performing organizations submit quarterly reports, though the information each PRO collects is slightly different. Both PROs will collect data about event dates, performers, venues, seating capacities, locations, the type of performance (e.g., free, benefit, or paid), gross revenue, and a copy of the program or a digital document with a list of repertoire. While many organizations are responsible about reporting their performances, composers should still remain diligent in also reporting performances to ensure all royalties are collected.

PROs and Traditional Publishing

While publishers are members of BMI or ASCAP and do occasionally report performances, this is more common with large-scale rental works, as these performances are easy to track and can generate a large amount of royalties for a publisher. Shorter works or those for smaller instrumentations, such as chamber pieces or choral octavo scores, may go untracked and unreported by traditional publishers. As mentioned above, it is in your best interest to track and report your performances whether they are self-published or traditionally published. As with other types of royalties, if you publish your work with a traditional publisher, you will typically forfeit half of your performing rights royalties. In that case, your PRO would split royalty payments equally between you and your publisher.

Direct Licensing

Another option—direct licensing—circumvents the need to decide which PRO to join. None of the composers interviewed mentioned exercising the option to direct-license their compositions, perhaps because so many composers are encouraged by their peers or mentors to join a PRO. Direct licensing works best if you hold the copyright to all aspects of the composition (e.g., words/lyrics, music, etc.) and you are licensing live performances of your works. You cannot directly license recordings of your music—say, a piece recorded and released by an ensemble and their respective label—unless you also hold the copyright to the master recording.

With a direct license, you skip the middle person (the PRO) and execute your own performing licenses with music users. In this way, you are not beholden to any strict or preestablished formulas; instead, you'll be setting your own rates. To determine a fee for direct licensing, establish a base rate, then adjust it for factors such as the type of usage (e.g., live performance, broadcast), audience size and/or capacity, frequency of use, and geographic reach. For example, the licensing fee for a local choral performance with an audience of two hundred might be significantly lower than the fee for a major symphony orchestra performance with two thousand audience members. Similarly, a national or regional broadcast would command a higher fee than a school radio station.

As with synchronization fees, no set rate or formula has been established for performing rights by any law, statute, or consent decree. You can negotiate a fee that you and the music user believe is reasonable. Some composers might negotiate a percentage of net ticket sales, whereas others might determine a flat rate depending on the type of ensemble (e.g., academic or non-academic), and the type of concert (e.g., a benefit concert versus a main-season performance). While there are many advantages to executing your own direct licenses, it does mean that you are taking on all of the work, whereas a PRO would be doing the bulk of that work for you. The trade-off is that you receive 100 percent of the licensing fees collected.

Because agreements with ASCAP and BMI are nonexclusive, you retain the right to direct-license any performance even if you do affiliate with a PRO. However, you'll want to avoid a scenario where your performance is direct-licensed through you *and* licensed through your PRO. In most cases, you will want to let your PRO contact know that you have direct-licensed a performance, so that they don't charge the presenter twice for the same performance. You can also work on this in partnership with the performing organization to prevent double-licensing.

Choosing a PRO

Many composers pick a PRO based on recommendations from peers and mentors. Julia Adolphe is grateful that she was told as an undergraduate to register with ASCAP or BMI, although, she says, "I was not given any sort of indication as to why [to choose] one or the other. I honestly chose randomly, and still have no idea if I made the right decision."

Choosing a PRO may feel like an ethical quandary or an arbitrary guess, but be assured that the differences between them are minimal. What matters most is that you start collecting performing royalties, whether that's through ASCAP, BMI, or direct licensing. "You want somebody to protect your catalog," Jeff Beal says. "How lucky are we that there's actually a corporation or an entity where their sole mission in life is to go out and monetize our catalogs, whether it's our performances in a concert hall or on streaming and media?"

Adding Up Your Income Streams

As you review these passive income streams, it may feel laughable to consider how little you may earn from any particular source. Shawn Kirchner urges composers to have the patience to allow their royalties to build and accumulate over time. "Until you have a certain number of pieces out there, you can't be generating the rolling income of royalties," he says. "There's a certain quantity and threshold number. Once you get enough different people performing your music in enough regions of the country, then you start to notice these little income streams that contribute to the river."

Many of the composers we spoke with recommended diversifying your income beyond commissions, though these admittedly make up the largest portion of many composing incomes. Active and passive income streams can ebb and flow. Kirchner notes that some years you may be invited to multiple residencies and guest appearances, but then you may receive none the following year. Juhi Bansal suggests that composers never want to be entirely reliant on any single source of income, since a combination of multiple income streams provides the safety net and the diversification in earnings that allows composers to weather slower seasons. Given that many composers already have experience performing, conducting, designing their own websites, editing recordings, or engraving polished scores, you may already have several new active income streams that you could add to your overall income portfolio right now.

On the other hand, your passive income streams may be quite low at the start. It is not uncommon to receive royalty checks for tens of dollars—or for less than ten dollars. As previously discussed, maintaining a healthy mindset in this career includes acknowledging what you can't control. Many possible composing income streams involve external and unpredictable factors. Just as investment bankers encourage clients to diversify their investment portfolios to weather uncertain or volatile market conditions, diversifying your income streams as a freelance musician allows you to maintain a stable income despite the inherent unpredictability of your career. Even if the amounts are low, remember Shawn Kirchner's words: over time, these small streams can contribute to a large river.

Remember, too, that your income streams do not have to relate directly to your compositional path. As Abbie Betinis shared in Chapter 5, she owns an investment property; being a landlord allows her to collect a monthly passive income. In 2006, Jocelyn Hagen and Timothy C. Takach cofounded Graphite Publishing, a company that publishes and distributes contemporary music. This company allows Hagen and Takach to advocate for and promote the work of contemporary composers—work that benefits their community—and also to generate passive income through score sales royalties. "Investing our time and money into Graphite was one of the smartest things we ever did," Hagen says. "It was a labor of love, and we didn't make money from it at first, but we didn't care." Hagen envisions the company as a kind of "machine that keeps spinning"—a benefit that will provide passive income in her retirement.

Just as passive income streams can free up your time and energy, hiring assistance with your career—in the form of an assistant, manager, publicist, copyist, engraver, bookkeeper, or accountant—can add further value to your composing life. Hiring help for your business and creative needs can grant you more time to compose, pursue other jobs or hobbies, or spend time with family and friends. The following chapter will address these and more advantages of hiring help with your composing career.

8
Assembling Your Team

As you progress in your career, you may find it increasingly challenging to manage every aspect of your professional life on your own. This is a good problem to have: it means you are growing. While some successful composers self-manage every aspect of their business, many more choose to employ help in the form of managers, agents, publicists, assistants, and engravers/copyists. This chapter describes the various professionals who can take some of the burden of managing your business off your plate, leaving you more time to be creative.

Knowing When to Hire Assistance

How do you recognize the right moment to hire help? For Jennifer Jolley, it's a quality-of-life issue: when you feel as though you can no longer keep up with your work, you'll know it is time to consider hiring outside assistance. For Melissa Dunphy, an assistant functions as a gatekeeper—what Dunphy calls a "buffer between me and personally interacting with every single person who emails me."

In 2005, after Eric Whitacre's music spread widely on peer-to-peer file sharing sites and demand for his work soared, he was receiving so many emails and offers that he needed someone to help oversee them. After working with a series of managers, Whitacre met his current manager, Claire Long, in 2008, when she was managing the King's Singers and he was writing a piece for the ensemble. He remembers thinking of Long as "intelligent and kind and tough," qualities that he believes make for a great manager.

After that initial collaboration, Whitacre asked Long if she'd oversee his conducting opportunities in Europe. "She wrote me back with several pages of: 'Here's what your career should be, and here's what we should do,'" he says. Within three weeks, he had hired her to oversee every aspect of his career. In recent years, Whitacre's team has grown to include an associate manager, Meg Davies. "I really don't take a breath without their counsel," he says.

Composing a Living. Brandon Elliott and Dale Trumbore, Oxford University Press.
© Brandon Elliott and Dale Trumbore 2025. DOI: 10.1093/9780197803509.003.0009

Once you've realized you are in the right position to hire assistance—you can't keep up with your workload yourself, and you have the financial resources to outsource some of your less-creative work—it's time to decide what kind of help would be most beneficial to you and your career.

Different Types of Support

Managers

As your career progresses, balancing your time and your workload becomes crucial. This is where a manager can help. Granted, the term "manager" can be confusing; there are different types of managers within the overall music industry. Most commonly, though, the term "manager" refers to a personal manager. A manager serves as your professional ally, prioritizing important tasks, organizing your schedule, and acting as a gatekeeper to prevent you from becoming overwhelmed. One day they may be negotiating a contract on your behalf, and the next day they're confirming travel arrangements for an upcoming residency.

Contrary to common misconception, managers are not in the business of procuring employment for you. That is technically—and in some states, legally—the role of an agent, which is discussed later in this chapter. Still, for some composers, the definitions of an agent and a manager may blur. For Julia Adolphe, management at its best looks like a partnership. "Especially as a composer," she says, this partnership is about "your relationships and their relationships, and approaching that from both angles." Adolphe has had mixed experiences working with managers. In one best possible outcome, though, her manager at the time pursued a connection with a top-name orchestra. Adolphe had already established rapport with many of the performers and donors of that ensemble, and her manager helped facilitate an introduction to the executive director. Together, Adolphe's connections and her manager's outreach led to a commission from the orchestra.

A manager can help you ask for more money or other perks that you wouldn't necessarily feel comfortable requesting yourself. "I remember when I had somebody negotiating my contracts for me, [collaborators] took me a little bit more seriously," Jennifer Jolley says. Hiring a manager has also been tremendously helpful for Derrick Skye, as that manager reminds him to charge what he's worth and value his time appropriately. "I definitely feel more valuable when I have someone else speaking on my behalf," Skye says.

Depending on whom you hire as your manager, you may find yourself paying a retainer fee (a set amount per month), an hourly rate, or a percentage of your gross revenue across all music-related activities. The percentage fee is negotiable, and can range from 10–25 percent, but most commonly will be around 15–20 percent for concert composers and closer to 12–15 percent for film composers. In this arrangement, your manager is paid "on commission," and if you earn nothing, you don't owe them any money. There is a mutual benefit to working together to maximize your career potential. This can also create some ethical and legal challenges, though, as your manager may pressure you to take on work that you don't want to do so they can earn their commission. This imbalance has led to the creation of laws in many states that distinctly divide the role of a manager and an agent.

Julia Adolphe's managerial woes began when her manager attempted to take on multiple roles, asking for commission-based payment, a portion of Adolphe's sales royalties, *and* a retainer fee. This manager sent her two contracts with two pricing models but failed to inform Adolphe it would be standard to sign only one. "One had a retainer fee and one had a commission structure," Adolphe says. "The way it was presented to me was that I needed to sign both."

Traditionally, Adolphe explains, publicists have a retainer fee and managers take a commission, though it is increasingly common to see management companies ask for both. "I made the mistake of having this manager explain the contract to me" instead of a lawyer, she says. Adolphe had prepared a long list of questions, and the manager answered them thoroughly. "But when I later consulted with a lawyer, it became clear that the [manager's] explanation did not line up with my understanding, and of course our conversation wasn't in writing, so [the manager] was able to go back and say, 'That's not what I said.'" That manager also contractually required a cut of Adolphe's sales royalties. This is standard for a publisher, but it is atypical for a management company.

Adolphe views her plight as a cautionary tale. "I wish there had been much more clarity around what to expect from managers, what to expect from publicists, what to expect from publishers, how royalties factor into all of that, and the different payment structures for those kinds of relationships." While Adolphe's manager had several major clients, none were composers, which could explain why her manager asked for rights and royalties that are usually reserved for publishers.

"There are specific challenges to composition and what a composer needs," Adolphe explains. "I've had three different managers, and I was either their only composer or one of two. A lot of the time I felt like I was trying to shift their model to fit what I needed, and that was challenging." Adolphe warns against working with managers who don't usually have composers for clients, who may in practice be used to booking performers (technically working as agents) rather than helping you facilitate relationships that lead to commissions.

Managers vs. Agents: What's the Difference?

Managers and agents serve distinct functions. Agents represent clients by seeking employment for them and are often regulated by state labor laws. California and New York have the most robust laws, given their deep involvement in the entertainment industry. At the time of publication, twenty-two states had laws to regulate the operation of talent agents, typically requiring a license to operate. Each state has varying levels of restrictions, and California is notorious for having the most restrictive regulations. For example, in California, any agency contract that talent is asked to sign must be pre-approved by the labor commissioner.

Agents are typically affiliated with either boutique or full-service agencies. Like managers, agents are often paid on a commission basis, with 10–20 percent being the industry standard. Unlike agents in other industries such as film and television, music agents do not typically provide overall career guidance for music talent. Their sole purpose is to book you opportunities. As a composer, those might be performances, workshops, residencies, or speaking engagements. It's also not uncommon to have more than one agent, with each specializing in a particular niche—one for speaking engagements and one for guest conducting, for example.

Whereas agents are heavily regulated by statute, managers are seldom regulated. You can technically have your agent also serve as your manager, but that may result in a higher commission fee structure. Laws forbid individuals from serving as both a manager and an agent for a client in New York and California, because this can create an inherent conflict of interest. Of the composers interviewed here, few work with agents, while many work with managers.

If you have a manager who is pitching your work to an orchestra, says Derrick Skye, "and you don't even know that they're pitching your work because you're off doing something else, and then the orchestra decides to do it, and they're going to give you $15,000 to $20,000—that [manager] got you that gig. I think that they deserve to be compensated for getting you $15,000 to $20,000." However, Skye notes, so far in his career, the only person getting him gigs has been . . . himself. "The manager's really just looking over contracts when I send them, or doing contract negotiation. If I'm the one actually getting the gig, and then they're doing admin work, then [their payment] is really just hourly. And so coming up with that hourly rate, that really is an agreement that you can make with your manager." As mentioned previously, managers working with composers may be paid on commission, by an hourly rate, or with a monthly retainer fee.

Angélica Negrón hired her current manager when she was overwhelmed with film and orchestral opportunities and feeling ill-equipped to negotiate those rates. "At that time, I was doing a lot of teaching artist work, too, which I loved," she says. The teaching work often intersected with her orchestral commissions; for example, this could take the form of a new commission that also included several community workshops. Negrón felt the commissioning fee and residency fee should be negotiated separately, but didn't know how to approach that. When she hired her manager, the manager asked for a list of her current projects, then helped Negrón manage her contracts and workflow.

Negrón notes that some composers assume she gets her opportunities because she has a manager seeking them out. (In other words, they assume her manager works as both manager *and* agent.) In actuality, her manager helps organize the opportunities that come to her by finding co-commissioners for pieces that don't have the full budget for a commission and discovering other ways to maximize opportunities.

"It's a lot of reacting to what's coming," Negrón says. "I also feel very lucky that I found her, because I've heard many stories of others [where] it was not a good fit. For composers, I think it's not as straightforward as a performer or a band to have a manager." Negrón recommends hiring additional help when you are taking on a project that feels out of your area of expertise. While you could hire an assistant or manager, that assistance could also look like hiring a producer, an accountant, or a librettist.

Film Scoring Agents

Dara Taylor notes that whereas an actor might move to Los Angeles and start their career path by finding an agent, this is far from the first step in a film composer's journey. Both Taylor and Jeff Beal note that finding a film composing agent can be complex, and it may take years of experience before you are signed with an agency. "I don't think you can decide when you have somebody represent you; it's when somebody wants to represent you," Beal says.

"It's very hard to get an agent unless you already have an established history of work."

Taylor calls it "a kind of chicken-or-the-egg" situation, where "you work with an agency to get work, but you need work to get an agent." She notes that she was fortunate to start forming a relationship with the same agency as her previous boss. Taylor became familiar with her current agent as she attended events like premieres with her former employer. After she had gained several years of experience and accolades, including a 2019 Hollywood Music and Media award, that agent offered to represent her. Getting an agent can be "a long process," Taylor says.

Both Beal and Taylor note that the standard rate for an agent in their field can range from 12–20 percent, with that rate varying for package deals versus composing fees. In Beal's experience, most agencies charge somewhere in the middle of that range; for example, a film agent may take a 12.5 percent cut on a package deal and 15 percent on a composer's fee. Beal, who composes both concert music and film music, notes that his agent never receives a cut of his performance or other concert music income. Taylor says her agent "pays for herself," citing one example where a film production offered an $8,000 fee and her agent successfully countered with a $10,000 rate.

Assistants

In the busy life of a composer, delegating tasks can be a game-changer. Assistants can help with various responsibilities and administrative tasks, which could include managing your email inbox, sending invoices and tracking due dates for payments, updating your website, or conducting research. Taking one or more of these tasks off your mind can allow you to allocate more time to your creative work.

It's rare to find an assistant who understands you and what you do right away. When hiring an assistant, prepare for an initial learning curve where you spend time training that person, allowing for some lost creative time in the process. Once you've trained them, though, you may easily free up several hours per week.

The wide spectrum of types of assistants you can hire and train ranges from virtual assistants (including people with little to no music experience) to college students (who may require more training at the start of your working relationship) to professionals with years of experience. A team member "can literally be anybody that has the ability to learn," Derrick Skye says. "You just need to sit down with them, and you need to teach them how you like to do things." Skye finds this approach "refreshing," noting that you can train an assistant or manager to create internal systems that help with your specific workflow.

Publicists and PR Firms

Public attention is the lifeblood of any composer's career, ensuring that your music reaches a broader audience. While you can do your best to generate a positive buzz about your music on your own, publicists specialize in crafting your public image, connecting you with the media, and promoting your music. This approach can, in turn, bring you more job opportunities.

Unfortunately, much like managers, there are not many publicity firms that specialize in working with composers. However, if you are at a point in your career where you need robust publicity or public relations support, many firms are used to working within the music industry. Your assistant or manager may also serve as your publicist.

Skye found his publicist through a referral outside of the music industry. "Hiring a PR firm to handle social media was a great starting point, because it helped me to learn everything necessary for maintaining a strong online presence," he says. "I saw how they set things up and gained a lot of valuable insights. . . . I figured out what needs to be done and how to do it through both observation and conversation." After the initial setup and expansion of Skye's social media presence, he shifted to an "as needed" arrangement with the firm, where they handled social media and PR on a case-by-case basis rather than on a regular schedule.

Composers should check their expectations to ensure they align with what a publicity or public relations firm will offer. Keep in mind that most contracts with PR firms will not guarantee any specific performance, metric, or outcome. It also generally takes several months for a PR firm to land substantial placements if you are an artist who has not had any previous coverage in major media or publications. Furthermore, in recent years, media budget cuts have resulted in fewer arts journalism outlets (and arts journalists) to pitch. If you don't have a compelling major project to promote and a distinct angle from which to pitch it, you may find that you are wasting money by hiring a publicist.

Still, some composers choose to hire a publicist on a project basis, retaining a publicist to promote a specific album release or several overlapping premieres. Molly Joyce says that for future recordings, if she had the resources,

"I'd look into probably hiring the best publicist I could get rather than looking at the best record label." Given that results are not guaranteed, a composer working on a longer-term basis with a publicist could easily spend as much as $20,000–30,000 before they saw any meaningful placements—if they saw placements at all.

If you are working with a larger institution like an orchestra, opera company, or big concert venue, you may be able to take advantage of their in-house publicist to promote your work. Skye's work *Song of the Ambassadors*—created in collaboration with K Allado-McDowell, who founded the Artists and Machine Intelligence initiative at Google, and data artist Refik Anadol—was reviewed in the *New York Times* Science and Technology section after its premiere at Lincoln Center. Skye was grateful that the science section accurately described the artificial intelligence that he and his collaborators explored in this project, noting that the review likely reached an even broader audience than if it had been covered in the music section. When you are considering whether to hire a publicist and how a project might be pitched to various news outlets, consider your project's non-musical elements as well as its musical ones. While arts journalism is dwindling, your publicist may be more successful pitching your project as a more wide-ranging article or profile than a straightforward music review.

Engravers and Copyists

Engravers and copyists can provide welcome assistance to composers. While the jobs they perform are slightly different, both can enhance the appearance and legibility of your scores and parts.

Engravers

Engravers help make your score look as clean on the page as possible, working from a handwritten score, editing a score you've prepared in notation software, or transcribing a score created in a digital audio workstation (DAW). An engraver will work with you to prepare a finished score that's ready for performance or publication.

Many composers choose to do their own engraving work, but if you compose primarily by hand or with a DAW, you may find it helpful to hire assistance engraving your scores. If you choose to publish your work with a traditional publishing house, they will also likely re-engrave your music into their preferred notation system—an expense that you will not be expected to cover.

Copyists

Copyists proofread and prepare music for performance, which often includes extracting and preparing individual performance parts from a full score. Copyists may or may not offer editing services; while some may report typos as they encounter them in parts preparation, others focus primarily on formatting.

While many early-career composers prefer to handle parts preparation themselves to save money, you may find that the time saved in hiring an engraver or copyist is extremely valuable. The act of preparing twenty or more parts in a large-ensemble work can be particularly tedious, and composers are often expected to hire a copyist for this work rather than do it themselves.

If you are negotiating a contract for a commission that features a large ensemble, like wind ensemble or orchestra, you'll likely be able to request reimbursement for hiring a copyist. This may also apply to works for smaller ensembles. The copyist fee should exist separately from your commissioning fee as an additional line item in your contract. Within the contract, the amount of the copyist fee may or may not be restricted. For example, you may see a clause like the following: "[Organization] will bear the costs of preparing and reproducing the parts and score" or "[Organization] agrees to pay for extraction, preparation, and copying of orchestral parts to the work, up to a maximum of $1,000.00 (one thousand dollars)." Note that you will likely have to forward your copyist's invoice along to the commissioning ensemble in order to be reimbursed for this cost. Even if you do choose to do the parts preparation yourself, you can still request reimbursement for this expense.

Accountants and Bookkeepers

Chapter 11 will discuss the distinct roles of accountants and bookkeepers, as well as the value they can bring to your team.

Investing in Your Team: Costs and Benefits

You may be concerned that expanding your team by hiring an assistant, engaging with a manager, or collaborating with any other professional will be prohibitively expensive. It is essential, though, to recognize that team expansion can offer tremendous value to your career. Only you can weigh your current budget against the potential gains offered by hiring assistance. When evaluating the potential costs and benefits, take the following factors into account.

Valuing Your Time

What is the true worth of an hour of your time? Only you can make that calculation, based on what you have been paid in the past and the value you place on your hours. If the value of your time is more than the cost of hiring support, then that investment becomes advantageous. For example, if you estimate your time's value at $40 per hour and you hire an assistant for $20 per hour for five hours a week, you'll save $200 in perceived value per week but will incur an expense of just $100. A manager may not necessarily do assistant work for you, but they will serve as a gatekeeper of your time, allowing you to focus on what matters to you while they handle other tasks.

Increased Productivity and Income

Delegating administrative and organizational tasks to a team member frees up more hours in your day. The additional hours can be devoted to your creative pursuits, which may involve composing, honing your musical skills through coaching or lessons, nurturing professional relationships, or generating innovative ideas. This surge in productivity could result in a higher volume of completed compositions—and a higher income—or an elevated standard of work. In the long run, the potential creative and financial benefits of freeing up your time can outweigh the initial cost, transforming it into a sound investment. If you hire an agent to bring in new work, they may also "pay for themself" via the jobs they help you secure or the increased pay rates they negotiate for you.

Maintaining Work-Life Balance

Achieving a harmonious work-life balance is an ongoing challenge for many composers. Expanding your team can allow you to define clearer boundaries around work and reserve time for personal and leisure activities like spending time with family, devoting time to your physical and mental well-being, or pursuing a hobby. Similarly, delegating tasks that lie beyond your expertise or are excessively time-consuming can significantly diminish the stress associated with this career. These stressful secondary responsibilities might include negotiating contracts, updating your website, or declining unwanted gigs—all tasks that can be outsourced.

Finding Help: Hiring Assistance

When you are ready to hire help with your career, "ask ask ask around," Shara Nova says. Cast a wide net as you solicit referrals from friends, mentors, and colleagues. Once you have a list of names in hand, ask the person or agency you are considering hiring to give you references in the form of a list of current or former clients. This list shouldn't be proprietary; for example, any manager with a satisfied client base should be willing to put you in touch with a happy client who can sing their praises. After Julia Adolphe's negative experiences with managers unaccustomed to working with composers, she recommends asking not only for references from satisfied clients, but from satisfied *composer* clients.

Deciding When to Move On

Let's say you do hire a new member of your team, but your communication styles aren't meshing. How do you know when the moment is right to let a team member go?

After Adolphe's first management experience went south, she was able to break her two-year contract. She hired a lawyer to help negotiate the terms of commissions that had been brokered through that manager; since many commissions are booked years ahead, Adolphe still had ongoing projects that would pay that manager royalties. With her subsequent managers, thirty days' notice was sufficient to end a working relationship. "I don't understand the two-year minimum" that some managers request, Adolphe says. "If the relationship is not working, it's in both parties' interests to sever ties."

Eric Whitacre describes knowing when to leave a manager as similar to knowing when to leave a relationship: while you may hesitate to break up, there's usually a moment when it will become clear to you that it isn't a good fit. When an early manager presented Whitacre with an opportunity to arrange what was essentially a thirty-second version of Beethoven's Ninth Symphony for a car commercial, Whitacre balked at the job, even though it would have paid what he calls "insane amounts of money." After a long, sleepless night asking himself what he truly valued, Whitacre realized that the job—and this manager—were not the right fit for him.

This is part of the risk of hiring a commission-based manager, who may be incentivized to push projects on you that will command a high price. "A good manager, actually, is thinking less about money and more about your career," Whitacre says, and a great manager will be "endlessly planting seeds" that five or ten years from now will "bloom and create opportunities." As a result of his successful, collaborative relationship with manager Claire Long and Meg Davies, Whitacre feels a sense of accountability. "Thankfully there are managers out there, like mine, with a shared sense of integrity and understanding of what we're trying to make—making money isn't the ultimate goal here."

No matter what, you must keep your own best interests in mind. Adolphe points out that one of her former managers knew nothing about copying expenses and how they need to be factored separately into an orchestral commissioning contract. "I explained that to him several times, and he still forgot," she says, "and so you have to sort of look out for yourself anyway."

Ways to Automate Your Work

In the age of digital innovation, you have access to a plethora of tools and technologies designed to streamline work processes and enhance efficiency. Automation is a powerful strategy to optimize your workflow and free up valuable time. Consider the following approaches, and see the Resources section for links to software that can help with these automation tactics.

Email Management

Email can be a time-consuming distraction. Use email management software to categorize and prioritize your messages, automatically sort them into folders, and even draft responses in advance. This way, you can focus your energies on essential emails while avoiding repetitive tasks.

Contact Management

There are software programs available that can read your emails, extract contact information, create new contacts or update existing ones, and search the internet for associated social media profiles. By automating these processes, you can maintain an organized and up-to-date contact list without manual effort.

Social Media Scheduling

Tools for scheduling social media posts allow you to plan and automate your online presence. You can compose posts in advance and set them to publish at specific times. This helps maintain an active online profile without the need for constant real-time engagement.

Project Management Software

Composers engaged in multiple projects can benefit from project management software. These platforms help you plan, track, and collaborate on projects efficiently. They can also automate reminders, timelines, and task assignments, reducing the risk of missed deadlines.

Financial Management

Utilize financial software or apps to automate financial tracking, invoicing, and expense management. These tools provide clear insights into your income and expenditures, saving you time on manual calculations and record keeping.

A Network of Support

Navigating the world of management, agents, publicists, assistants, engravers, and copyists is an exciting phase of your career. Building your support team and embracing automation are not mutually exclusive; in fact, they can complement each other effectively. The key is to strike a balance that aligns with your unique needs and goals. Your support team can provide invaluable human assistance, opening doors to opportunities and enhancing your efficiency. Simultaneously, the judicious use of automation tools empowers you to streamline your workflow, reduce repetitive tasks, and make the most of your time. Whether you are just beginning to explore these options or you are considering expanding your team, you have multiple options for building a solid support system.

9

Transitioning to 100 Percent Freelance Composing

Music composition is an incredibly challenging career in which to make a full-time living through freelancing, and almost half of the composers interviewed here observed that full-time freelance composing was not the best fit for them. If you are contemplating a freelance composing career, you are likely facing a number of questions:

- If I want to support myself fully with only money made from composing, how do I make that transition?
- When composing jobs arrive sporadically and in unpredictable amounts, how do I make a stable living for myself?
- Is it possible to support a family on a freelance composing income?
- What do I do if no new jobs are coming in?

This chapter will address those concerns and help you decide whether freelance composing is a good fit for you. While freelancing comes with numerous challenges, balancing part- or full-time work alongside a composing career can be just as difficult. Jennifer Jolley acknowledges that teaching expends both her time and energy, so she tries to negotiate the balance between her job requirements and her composing career. "How much energy do I spend teaching and grading, and how much time do I spend composing?" she asks herself. "I'm working on that balance. It is elusive, but I try."

Many composers, like Jolley, rely on income from teaching or performing to supplement their composition income. This provides stability through several factors—a steady paycheck, health insurance, and a retirement plan—that a freelance career lacks. Understanding the trade-offs of either path will help you make the best decision for your career.

Composing a Living. Brandon Elliott and Dale Trumbore, Oxford University Press.
© Brandon Elliott and Dale Trumbore 2025. DOI: 10.1093/9780197803509.003.0010

Full-Time or Part-Time Composing: What's Right for You?

Freelance composing may *not* be the right path for you if:

- You have no interest in cultivating multiple passive and active income streams.
- You much prefer a stable source of income, health insurance, and an employer-provided 401(k) or pension.
- You would rather not put pressure on your art to provide financial support as well as creative fulfillment.

It may take a certain type of personality to make a full-time freelance living writing music. You need a genuine interest, or even enjoyment, of the business side of this career. If you don't find the business aspects we've outlined in previous chapters compelling—factors like navigating different active and passive income streams, building your network, hiring assistance, and more—there's nothing wrong with that.

On the other hand, freelance composing may be the right path for you if:

- You love the idea of building your life around composing full-time.
- You are comfortable hustling to find and create your own opportunities, which will necessarily include fostering relationships with potential collaborators.
- You can live with the uncertainty of not knowing exactly when your next job will come in.
- You find the business elements of a composing career interesting, and you are eager to learn how to build your business in a sustainable way.
- You are willing to become financially literate when it comes to elements traditionally provided by an employer, including opening your own retirement account(s) and potentially covering your own health insurance.

Why Consider Full-Time Freelancing?

For some composers, full-time freelancing is the dream. Freelance composers control how they allocate their hours: they can choose to work forty hours a week or opt for a more relaxed work schedule. They have flexible and theoretically limitless vacation time. They may be able to work from anywhere in the world, as long as they have access to the right instruments and/or composing software. Most important, full-time freelance composers spend every day with the craft of composing: the business side of it, yes, but also the sheer joy of writing music whenever they'd like. For some composers, this is the ultimate definition of success: a life spent making art.

If you aspire to compose full-time, though, how do you make the jump to an unpredictable lifestyle? How do you weigh the economics of this decision, balancing financial instability with the desire to control your own time? And how do you start preparing for the transition to full-time composing years before you are actually ready to make that leap?

Composer Juhi Bansal recently made the move to composing full-time. "I know what the stable teaching path looks like," she says. "I've done it. I know its downfalls very well, as well as its upsides." Bansal doesn't consider herself the kind of person who naturally gravitates toward the risks of a freelance career. But having seen the downsides of a more traditional, steady path as a composition professor, Bansal is much more open to freelance composing. She also notes that she has worked a variety of different jobs. "If or when things are slow, [those jobs are] always something I know I can fall back on. . . . Realistically, life happens, and you have to branch out sometimes." To tell composers otherwise—to present them with any single model of success, including one that doesn't include a fallback plan—is doing them a disservice.

The common expression "leap and the net will appear" is misleading and misguided, especially when it comes to building a financially stable freelance career. Freelance composers should build their "safety net" first, ideally over a period of five to ten years, before they "leap." But what goes into building an infrastructure for your creative life—a system that will ensure you can thrive as a freelance composer?

Prepare for Uncertainty

The unpredictability of a freelance career can actually work in your favor, allowing you to shape your career on your own terms. Chapter 7 discussed how to diversify your income streams so that if one dries up, you are prepared to strengthen other income sources and support yourself. In addition to cultivating diverse income sources and building wealth, you'll need to identify what is required to sustain your cost of living.

Track your expenses for a month: what amount will cover your rent or mortgage, groceries, utilities, insurance costs, phone bill, internet, and other charges? What, additionally, do you want to be saving each month and putting toward an emergency fund as well as retirement income? When you have a target number for your income goal—even if that number feels unreasonably steep—you can begin to assess how composing income might cover those costs.

One pitfall of freelance composing is the reality of never knowing when your payments will come in. Some income sources, like PRO royalty payments, arrive annually or quarterly, but you may not know whether to expect a paycheck for hundreds or thousands of dollars or nothing at all. Similarly, score sales royalties usually peak around the academic calendar, particularly for composers who write works for collegiate and K–12 ensembles. For these ensembles, score sales royalties may spike in August and January, as new semesters begin. Still, the exact amounts of the royalties are unpredictable, and if you work with a traditional publisher or distributor, you may not receive payment for those sales until later in the fall or spring.

Out of the many sources of composing income, commissions are both the easiest to track and the most challenging to anticipate, as you have little control over when a new composing gig will arrive. Standard concert music commissioning contracts dictate payment in two or more installments, including an initial payment upon signing a contract and another when the piece is complete. Film contracts often split this payment into thirds, as mentioned in Chapter 6.

Once you've secured a commissioning contract, you can account for those two or more payments arriving in a more-or-less timely manner. However, you may find that collaborators are sometimes delayed in paying you. Academic institutions can be particularly lax in paying composers on time, especially when a payment must be approved by several administrators before it arrives in your bank account. Luckily, more organizations inside and outside of academia are moving to a direct deposit model, which can result in quicker and more predictable payments for composers.

When you are mapping out your anticipated income for the year, leave a two-month window in which to actually receive the money you are owed. If your contract stipulates that a collaborator has a thirty-day grace period in which to pay you, you may not know that they've forgotten about your fee until the grace period has already passed—though you can certainly follow up sooner to ensure that your payment has been processed. Track these payments and their due dates. If money does not arrive within thirty days of invoicing an ensemble, be ready to send a prompt follow-up inquiry about that payment.

Build Your "Safety Net"

As you consider the move to freelance composing, build a "safety net" of three to six months' worth of income saved in a readily accessible emergency fund. Start building this fund long before you plan to make the jump to freelance work, even if you plan to keep a part- or full-time job on the side. Some composers find it helpful to automate their savings so that a certain amount is moved from their checking account to their emergency fund on a monthly or weekly basis. This money will help when unexpected events, like a sudden illness or a global pandemic, prevent you from earning income.

"Something I started doing very early on is reminding myself of that uncertainty and always saving for a rainy day," Sydney Guillaume says. When Guillaume gets a big check, he puts some of the money away for estimated taxes and some away in an emergency fund. When he recently decided to take a sabbatical, the fund helped to support him while he figured out his next steps. "I don't like to live paycheck to paycheck," Guillaume says. "It's been a while since that happened. It's an uncomfortable feeling, and it also affects your creativity."

Don't commit to full-time freelancing until you have a firm grasp on how much money you'll need to sustain your lifestyle. If you set a goal date for your jump to full-time freelance work, make it a flexible one. Your anticipated composing income and the strength of your emergency fund have the power to move that date forward or back.

Privilege in Composition

Privilege can be a significant factor in allowing composers more flexibility in their careers. Many full-time freelance composers have external support in the form of a spouse or partner who makes a high salary and/or provides access to health care. Others may receive assistance from their families in the form of a down payment on a house or help with childcare, rent, and other expenses. Some composers have access to a family trust fund, which allows them greater freedom with their time.

It's important to acknowledge this inherent inequity, especially since it is often invisible. When you see a composer working as a full-time freelancer, there may be unseen factors making that lifestyle more viable for them. If full-time freelancing is a goal of yours but you're ultimately not in the financial position to meet it, this is not a moral failing on your part. Your ability to make a full-time living writing music is not a reflection on your talent. Make the most of the resources you do have, especially the ones with the greatest non-monetary value: your unique skills and your network of trusted collaborators.

Preparing for the Leap

Before you make a jump to full-time freelancing, consider your own financial factors: do they work for you or against you? Again, be scrupulous in tracking your annual composing income as well as your monthly expenses. If you are thinking about making the jump to freelancing, maintain full- or part-time work until your composing income is well within the amount you need to provide for yourself and/or your household.

Some composers, like Kile Smith, only turned to a full-time freelance career later in life. For thirty years, Smith worked for the Free Library of Philadelphia's Fleisher Collection of Orchestral Music. He started his work there as a music copyist, then became a supervisor, and was eventually promoted to curator. He also worked at WRTI, Philadelphia's listener-supported jazz and classical radio station, hosting a radio show of discoveries from the Fleisher collection and eventually becoming an on-air classical host.

"In 2011, I turned 55," Smith says. "I could retire from the library. So my wife and I sat down to figure out: Could we afford to do this?" Smith ultimately did retire from his nine-to-five job, keeping his part-time radio job until 2017. He used his newly free days to focus more of his time and energy on his composition.

Overcoming Obstacles to a Freelance Composing Career

Another hurdle in the way of freelance composing is time management. It can be tricky to define boundaries around free time as a full-time freelancer. Suddenly, you are the only one holding yourself accountable for finishing a project. If you find yourself struggling to stay on top of work emails and meet your deadlines in a timely manner, you might find that freelance composing is not for you.

In a freelance composing career, you are also the only one responsible for ensuring that you take healthy breaks and aren't overworking to the point of exhaustion. Timothy C. Takach notes that he has to set boundaries for his full composing schedule to ensure that he's not working all the time. He has to tell himself, "No, you know what? I've earned it today. I'm going to go read a book.

I'm going to go play a video game or watch a movie or whatever I want to do, because I had a full work day already."

Parenting While Composing

As a freelance composer, Jocelyn Hagen says being a parent is "motivating." Her children inspire her to "work harder so that I can give them the things that they want" and give them a high-quality life. Scheduling your working career around the needs of your household, though, can prove trickier with a freelance career than a more traditional job.

For Takach, becoming a parent actually helped structure his work day rather than restricting it. "Having my boys' school day define my work day helped me compartmentalize work versus life balance," he says. As a parent, he doesn't have the same kind of flexibility as childless freelance composers. He also no longer has the luxury of waiting to be inspired, then dropping everything to compose. But when his sons started having a regular routine, that helped Takach organize his work day around their schedule. For the most part, he works when his children are at school and takes breaks when his sons take breaks.

Isaac Io Schankler, another composer-parent who balances their composition work with a full-time teaching job, notes that it helps to break up their work into smaller chunks. As a parent, "it's harder to come by those long work blocks to compose. But if I can block off three or four hours, I can still get a lot done if I'm in the right frame of mind," Schankler says. They also find that an external deadline, or even a friend expecting a certain amount of progress made on a piece by a given date, is very helpful. "If I don't have that [deadline], I am far more likely to push that [composing] down to a lower priority for something that does have a more immediate deadline or consequence, whether it's teaching or parenting-related."

Leap Gradually, Not All at Once

For many freelancers, the "leap" to full-time composing is more likely to be a series of gentle, tentative steps. It will likely take years rather than months to make the transition, so plan to phase out your non-composing work gradually rather than all at once. Ensure that you have a steady stream of new work coming in. You may also want to wait to make that "leap" until you are booked with commissions at least a year out.

Early-career composers often wonder how to calculate how long a project will take. This mental math is important, especially when you are booking projects spanning the next year or more. The more you compose, the better sense you'll have of how long it takes you to complete a project of any scope: Can you write a three- to five-minute chamber work in a month, or do you need longer? What about a ten-minute orchestral work? How long does it take you to score a short film versus a feature?

Composers Julia Adolphe and Reena Esmail have had success tracking their composing hours in a spreadsheet. With this system, they calculate the exact number of hours it takes them to write each piece, gaining useful data they then use to estimate their average composing hours for works of various lengths and instrumentations. Composers who track their hours may also calculate their commissioning fees based on how much estimated time a project will require.

You may want to try something similar, keeping a spreadsheet like the one in Table 9.1 where you log all of your composing hours for each new piece. To keep the math simple, let's assume the table refers to the composing hours it took to write a three-minute prelude for piano titled *Piano Prelude 1*.

This data can be particularly helpful as you estimate how many average days, weeks, months, or even years you require to compose pieces of varying lengths and instrumentations. For example, if the composer of *Piano Prelude 1* was asked to compose a ten-minute work for solo piano, they could logically estimate that it would take them about seventeen days of composing at the same rate. Based on their table, it takes them an average of 5.75 composing hours to write each minute of solo piano music. If they need to devote 57.5 total composing hours to writing a ten-minute solo piano piece and their average rate is 3.45 composing hours a day, it will take them approximately 16.7

Table 9.1 Piano Prelude 1: Log of Composing Hours

Composing Date	Hours Spent Composing
July 20	1.25
July 24	5.5
July 25	3
July 30	4
August 2	3.5
Total hours spent composing	17.25
Total days spent composing	5 days, composing approximately 3.45 hours per day.

composing days to write that work. Of course, they may not compose for seventeen consecutive days. Composers calculating their approximate total project hours may factor in rest days, sick days, and other potential delays.

The example in Table 9.1 addresses composing for only one instrument, and writing a minute of music for solo piano will likely take you much less time than writing (and orchestrating) a minute of music for a larger ensemble. It may be helpful to log your hours composing for different sizes and/or genres of music so that you have a more accurate reference point as you schedule your commissions. In setting a deadline for a new work, allocate more time for bigger projects. As previously discussed, always pad your timeline to allow for unanticipated delays.

Timothy C. Takach takes a different approach to determining his composing schedule and setting appropriate rates, calculating how much money he needs to make every month to support himself and his family. He then uses that monthly number to determine what he needs to make on an average business day. This model doesn't include working on weekends, so his monthly estimate includes about twenty working days per month. That number in turn gives him a starting point for how much to charge for composer residencies and other gigs based on a daily rate. Of course, there's also what Takach calls "a magical sauce—that sort of untouchable element of who you are and what you bring that nobody else can, and that will eventually raise your price above that hourly rate."

To replicate Takach's process, you would begin by adding up all of your average monthly expenses, as in Table 9.2. In this example, if your monthly expenses totaled $4,300 and you worked approximately twenty days a month, you would need to make at least $215 a day ($4,300/20 = $215). You can then use this number to determine your day-rate to clinic with an ensemble (no less than $215) and your commissioning rate. If it takes you about a month (20 working days) to complete a five-minute commission, for example, you could

Table 9.2 Sample Monthly Expenses

Expense	Cost per Month
Rent or mortgage	$2,000
Groceries and restaurants	$1,000
Utilities	$500
Insurance	$500
Miscellaneous	$300
Total per month	**$4,300**

consider charging at least $4,300 for that project. Of course, as Takach notes, nothing is stopping you from charging *more* than you need to get by, especially as you notice an increasing demand for your work.

As Dale Trumbore built her own "safety net" over a period of ten years, starting in graduate school, she supplemented her composing income by nannying, editing scores for a small music publisher, and teaching piano. She purposefully chose part-time jobs that she could scale up or down in hours as needed, first dropping her nannying and editing gigs, then eventually cutting her piano studio back to ten students, then five, before letting go of that job entirely. She also saved up six months' worth of living expenses before making the leap to full-time freelance composing. Now, she schedules commissions up to two years into the future, allowing her to approximate when larger commissioning payments will arrive in her bank account.

As a full-time freelance composer, Trumbore approximates her annual income based on a blend of income streams—commissions, guest lecturing, mechanical licensing fees, PRO royalties, and score sales. While she saves for retirement in accounts like a Solo 401(k) and a Roth IRA, her spouse's job covers her health insurance, a cost she doesn't have to factor into her yearly expenses. She and her spouse also divide the cost of their mortgage, food expenses, and utilities, while her spouse pays for their property taxes and unexpected home repairs. Whenever Trumbore's bank account is looking low or there's a gap in her commissioning schedule, she initiates commissioning consortiums or reaches out to her network with proposals for future collaborations, allowing her some agency in how and when she is paid.

Investing in Your Network

Agency within a career—the freedom to initiate new collaborations, thus maintaining some control over when new projects arrive at your doorstep—comes from investing not only in your bank account, but in your network. A sustainable freelance career is only possible when you've cultivated relationships with trusted collaborators. These are the people who will be first in line to join a new consortium, and they are the collaborators whom you can approach with a compelling new project proposal.

During the COVID-19 pandemic, Dale Trumbore saw $25,000 of income disappear in a week. Two commissioning prospects for which she hadn't yet signed a contract vanished, as these two conductors were (rightfully) unwilling to commit to uncertain performance dates. Two college residencies, through which she would have made several thousand dollars in speaking fees, were also canceled. One of the few new commissions Trumbore did receive in 2020 came from a collaborator she'd already been working with for eight years, whom she considers a friend as well as a trusted colleague.

Your professional relationships are every bit as worthwhile as an emergency fund. The jump to a freelance career requires a diverse array of income streams, an emergency fund, *and* a network of close collaborators.

Be Ready to Market Your Work

In considering the shift to full-time freelancing, you'll also want to consider how you are promoting your music. Ask yourself the following questions, which can help you identify how to position yourself and your music within the market:

- What sets your music apart from that of your peers?
- What values are you promoting in your work?
- Is your work synonymous with quality in craft?
- Who is your target audience—the conductors, soloists, listeners, or other collaborators most likely to purchase and commission your work?
- Just as important, who is your music *not* intended for?

Juhi Bansal notes that in school, many composition teachers focus almost exclusively on building your craft. While a solid knowledge of your craft is key to writing great music, Bansal had no idea when she graduated with a doctorate that she also needed to have a plan to market her music: "It's not optional. It's completely essential. And none of building your craft is going to come to anything if you don't have all of that in place, too." You need to have the craft, she says, as well as everything else that makes up a viable business, including marketing and a brand identity.

"It felt like a weirdly large hurdle to leap," Bansal says, to put that branding plan in place and declare: "I'm selling myself. I'm trying to make an identity as a composer." But now, having worked as a freelance composer for several years, she acknowledges that self-marketing does get easier, especially if you redefine marketing for yourself as simply connecting with other musicians and listeners who share your interests.

Is Freelancing Right for You?

As a freelance composer, you'll be expected to promote, market, and speak about your work. You'll also be responsible for securing funding for your work, whether that's through commissions, consortiums, or grants. (See the Resources section for recommendations for further reading on marketing, public speaking, and grant writing.)

Consider your strengths and weaknesses. Jumping from part- to full-time freelance composing may or may not be a good fit for your career, and the only person who can make that decision is you. Many musicians who work other jobs alongside their composing take comfort in the fact that there's no financial pressure on their art: they will never have to take on paid composing work that they don't want. A full-time job outside composition affords these artists the luxury of writing only the music they want to compose, when they want to compose it.

Shawn Kirchner balances jobs as a church musician and singer with his composing career. He acknowledges that he prefers to hand off certain parts of his business, like score sales, to others. While contemporary composers don't need to rely on traditional publishers to make or break a career—a positive evolution in composing—Kirchner believes that some composers are fundamentally disinclined to run their own business.

Kirchner believes that many composers internalize the idea that they "can be good at everything: 'I can be super creative, super inspired, and really good at bookkeeping.'" But even given all of the resources that allow composers to run their own businesses—including self-publishing, social media, and personal websites—freelance composing still might not be the best choice for composers who are averse to treating composing as a business. For Kirchner, hiring assistance with running his business and choosing to publish more of his music traditionally has been helpful in freeing up not only his time, but also his mental capacity to write music.

Kirchner also finds personal meaning and community in his jobs as a church musician and performer. This, too, is an important consideration as you decide whether making a living as a full-time composer is the best way to lead a fulfilling life: would holding one or more jobs outside composition grant you more personal satisfaction? Many music educators teach not only because they enjoy a dependable salary and benefits, but because they find teaching rewarding. While balancing two or more jobs can be challenging, as Jennifer Jolley mentioned at the start of this chapter, that balancing act can be worthwhile if it provides meaning and fulfillment alongside your salary.

Deciding whether to pursue a job as a full-time freelance composer may come down to how much you actually enjoy the business side of this career. For composers like Alex Shapiro, running a business is almost as compelling as writing music. Pursuing a freelance composing career provides a sort of thrill—a logic puzzle to be solved. "I love a good contract," Shapiro says. "I love a good spreadsheet . . . but many people are not necessarily going to enjoy it as much. And if you don't enjoy something, you're not going to do it well, or you're not going to do it promptly—you're going to keep putting it off." When Shapiro is talking to composers who are trying to decide whether to remain self-published or sign their work with a publisher, she asks them, "When [score] orders come in, how do you feel about that? And when you have to print up invoices and package scores and set up distribution deals and all that stuff—How do you feel about it?"

While Shapiro confesses that she's not a "morning person," she does bound out of bed in the morning looking forward to getting back to work in her composing studio and seeing what new score orders have come in. "I spend the first four, sometimes longer hours of my day running my business," she says, and she saves the latter part of the day into the evening for composition. But even Shapiro, who loves the business aspect of her career, admits that this schedule might not appeal to everyone. Not all composers will share her enthusiasm for running a business alongside their composition. If that's not for you, Shapiro says, "there's nothing wrong with that."

10

Navigating Copyright, Contracts, and Legal Basics

Brandon Elliott knows that his music students' eyes glaze over as soon as the topic of copyright law is brought up. But every time you create music, you are interacting with copyright law. The better you understand these laws, the easier it will be to protect your work and ensure that you receive fair recognition and compensation for your music. You owe it to yourself to have a fundamental understanding of copyright law, your exclusive rights, and how you can benefit monetarily from those rights.

Many musicians assume that we must "lawyer up" as soon as we encounter even the most basic legalese. In reality, so long as you are acting responsibly, you will very rarely need an attorney. In some circumstances, though, you will absolutely want to consult a lawyer, and this is especially true as you encounter high-value contracts. This chapter will discuss the basics of copyright law as it pertains to intellectual property and contracts, as well as your options when a contract is breached. Note that while this chapter has been reviewed by a lawyer and paralegal for accuracy, nothing here should be construed as legal advice, as every set of circumstances is different. Still, the goal of this chapter is to leave you feeling more comfortable reviewing a written agreement, entering into negotiations, and holding yourself and your collaborators accountable whenever you sign a contract.

Understanding Copyright

"When I talk to young composers and they're learning about copyright," Eric Whitacre says, "at best, they think it's about the ownership of the title, but they also don't realize that that [copyright] can be used. If you give away your copyright, the publisher owns all of the rights to that piece, potentially in perpetuity. This model is painful for composers and feels outdated, but it continues to this day."

Composing a Living. Brandon Elliott and Dale Trumbore, Oxford University Press.
© Brandon Elliott and Dale Trumbore 2025. DOI: 10.1093/9780197803509.003.0011

US copyright law provides legal protection for various forms of intellectual property, including music. This protects your original musical compositions, lyrics, and sound recordings. To obtain copyright protection for your musical work, it must meet two criteria: *originality* and *fixation*. *Originality* means the work has been independently created and displays at least a minimal level of creativity. *Fixation* refers to the work being fixed in a tangible form, like printed or handwritten sheet music, a digital file, or a recording.

Dismantling Copyright Myths

Some composers still believe that sending yourself a certified mail copy of a score legally functions as a registration of copyright. It does *not*. This cannot substitute for a formal US Copyright Office registration and is entirely irrelevant to the question of ownership.

However, you don't need to register your work with the US Copyright Office in order to hold the copyright. Copyright protection exists automatically upon creation, though formal registration with the Copyright Office does provide additional benefits (discussed below). Furthermore, registering a self-published work does not prohibit you from later publishing a piece traditionally and transferring the copyright to the publisher. Note that if you choose to publish a piece traditionally, your publisher will typically register the copyright under the publisher's corporate name. There are a few exemptions to the automatic granting of copyright protection—work for hire and transfer of copyright or ownership—which this chapter will later address.

Fair Use and Infringement

Under copyright law, you, the copyright holder, have a number of rights: the exclusive right to reproduce and distribute your music, prepare derivative works, perform the music publicly, and display it publicly. These rights are subject to certain limitations and exceptions, such as fair use. Fair use allows for limited use of copyrighted material without permission in certain circumstances, such as for criticism, commentary, news reporting, teaching, or research. The definition of fair use is continually tested in courts, especially when it comes to artificial intelligence.

Infringement of copyright occurs when someone violates one or more of your exclusive rights without proper authorization. As copyright owner, you could then seek legal remedies, including damages and injunctions, to enforce your rights and protect your intellectual property. As mentioned above, this is why you may want to take the additional step of registering your work with the US Copyright Office: The strength of your legal argument will be informed by whether or not your copyright is formally registered. Here are some other advantages of registering your music with the US Copyright Office.

Registering Your Work with the US Copyright Office

Legal Evidence

Registration serves as legal evidence of ownership and copyright validity. In a dispute or infringement claim, a copyright registration provides a clear record of your ownership. This can make it easier to prove your rights in a court of law.

Statutory Damages and Attorney's Fees

If your work is registered before an infringement occurs or within three months of publication, you may be eligible to seek statutory damages and attorney's fees in a lawsuit. Statutory damages can allow you to recover a predetermined amount of damages (money) without the need to prove the actual financial losses caused by the infringement.

Enhanced Protection and Deterrence

The registration of your work acts as a deterrent against potential infringers. It helps establish a stronger position in enforcing your rights. In cases of willful infringement, where the infringer knowingly, intentionally, or recklessly violates your copyright, registering the work in advance can increase the potential damages you could be owed.

International Protection

While copyright protection exists automatically upon creation, registration with the US Copyright Office can be beneficial for international protection. The United States has reciprocal copyright agreements with many other countries, and registration can help facilitate enforcement and protection of your music worldwide.

Many of the composers interviewed here have not registered their works with the US Copyright Office. It can be time-intensive to submit every piece you write, and registering your music can become costly over time. Furthermore, there are few existing cases within the *classical* music industry where infringement cases ended up in a courtroom, though there have been some. Infringement cases are much more common in genres such as pop and rock. Overall, though, registering your self-published music with the US Copyright Office provides tangible benefits by offering additional legal protections, facilitating enforcement actions, and potentially increasing the damages you can seek if your copyright is violated. It's a valuable step for creators to safeguard their rights and maintain control over their intellectual property. Whether you choose to formally register is up to you, but there are obvious benefits to registration if you have the time and money.

The issue of keeping your copyright is just one of many crucial considerations when you enter into a contract with a collaborator. Contract law is both immense and fundamental; it's one of the first courses that law students take. In the following section, we'll highlight the key elements of a music contract, alert you to red flags to watch out for, and share stories from creators whose contracts either enhanced or disrupted their career path.

Navigating Contracts

Contract law governs the formation, interpretation, and enforcement of agreements between parties. At its core, a contract is a legally binding agreement that establishes the rights and obligations of those parties. Contrary to common belief, a contract does not necessarily need to be a formal written agreement. It could be as simple as an email exchange, a text message conversation, or even a handshake agreement. For Alex Shapiro, a great contract elucidates many possible scenarios with descriptive language in a very brief sentence. "You want to enunciate and make it extremely clear what rights you have," she says, "which is hopefully a lot of them, worldwide, in perpetuity."

Outlining an Offer, Acceptance, and Consideration

For a contract to be valid, it generally requires an *offer*, *acceptance*, and *consideration*—something of value exchanged between the parties—as well as the intention to create legal relations. The terms of the contract should be clear, certain, and capable of being enacted. If one party breaches the contract by failing to fulfill their obligations, the non-breaching party may seek remedies such as damages or specific performance (a legal term that means fulfillment of the contract as promised). Contract law aims to provide predictability, fairness, and enforceability in business transactions and personal agreements.

That may all sound incredibly formal, but as long as those three elements are present—*offer*, *acceptance*, and *consideration*—you likely have the legal foundation of a contract. Brandon Elliott's law colleague often jokes that going to a fast food restaurant meets this legal foundation: First you *order* something. Then the employee receives and *accepts* the order. The *consideration* is your payment, which is exchanged for your food.

If the fast food restaurant gives you the wrong order—regardless of intentionality—there is a contract breach. Is this type of contract breach going to carry any weight in a courtroom? Probably not, but it illustrates that we all enter into contractual agreements far more often than we might realize. The actual enforceability of a contractual agreement, however, depends on its formality and documentation.

The consideration portion of a contract—the value exchanged—doesn't necessarily have to be monetary. Still, "even if there's no money exchanged," Angélica Negrón says, "contracts are so important." In any collaboration—even if you are composing music for a friend's short film in exchange for a slice of pizza—you should still consider writing out a letter of agreement stating the terms to which you've both agreed. If the collaboration goes wrong, you'll have a record of your intentions and the agreement you both accepted.

Hiring a Lawyer

With a more formal contract—think tens of thousands of dollars and a multi-page agreement, versus a single pizza slice—some music creators may feel rightly intimidated. When is it time to call a lawyer? Can you ask the other party to change one or more of the clauses? What's your potential risk if you or the other party breaks the rules of the contract?

These are all great questions. If you have the financial resources to pay an attorney to review your contracts and provide legal advice, there's certainly no harm in doing so. But many music creators just starting out may not have the resources to pay an average of $450 per hour to have a contract reviewed or get a half-hour consultation.

Negrón acknowledges that lawyer fees can be intimidating. "It adds up quickly for artists," she says. But in Negrón's experience, using a lawyer is "more about consulting with someone that knows [the law], so you don't get burned in not knowing legal language. It's about finding what's right for you and also being strategic." In addition, hiring a lawyer just once can generate a template that can be adapted for future collaborations or text permissions.

Julia Adolphe considers hiring a lawyer to be even more essential than hiring a manager. Adolphe often composes for orchestra, with commissioning fees that can total tens of thousands of dollars. Given her past experiences with unfavorable contract terms, Adolphe considers hiring a lawyer well worth the expense, so long as the legal fees are less than 10 percent of her total commissioning fee. Granted, if your commissioning contracts are for smaller amounts, you may not deem it necessary or valuable to hire a lawyer at this point in your career.

Having an attorney look over your contracts before you sign can be especially valuable when you are working with a kind of contract that's new to you or particularly densely worded. Shapiro explains that in one hour of an attorney's time, they'll very likely catch things you won't, no matter how familiar you are with contracts. The money you invest in a lawyer's time could save or make you "thousands of dollars in the long run," she says. Even after years of working with legal input, Shapiro still has an attorney review her contracts. She suggests that you develop and use your own commissioning template, offering that to commissioners and choosing that option whenever you are given the choice between a commissioning party's contract or your own.

Determining Commissioning Contract Terms

No two contracts are or should be the same, so it's impossible to provide a one-size-fits-all template here. Still, while every commissioning contract is different, most have several clauses in common. In conversations with your commissioner, consider using the following questions as a starting point to determine your contract terms. You may not find all these questions relevant to every project—and some projects will require terms beyond those addressed here—but the outcome of the questions you do ask will help determine your contract terms.

To determine the **deadline** and **premiere date**, consider the following (or similar) questions about timeline:

- "What timeframe do you have in mind for the project?" This more general question can lead to the conversation points below.
- "What is the anticipated premiere date?" This may be an inexact date—a month or a season rather than a specific date—but having an idea of when the premiere will take place will allow you to plan an appropriate deadline with respect to your other work, prepare for potential travel to the premiere, and determine an appropriate exclusivity period (addressed in more detail below).
- "What is the anticipated deadline for the new piece?" Note that your *contractual* deadline may or may not match your *internal* deadline for the completion of a project. For example, if you have two pieces due the same week, you may wish to schedule one internal deadline for two months earlier, allowing yourself enough time to complete both compositions without unnecessary time pressure.
- "Are you hoping to see an early draft of the piece, or would you prefer for me to send you the completed piece?" Some composers offer a review period in which a conductor can review a near-final draft of the piece and offer initial feedback. If this is something you'll offer, consider placing a term limit on this feedback period: two weeks, for example, in which the commissioner can review the draft and offer their feedback, after which you will incorporate their notes, finish the work, and deliver the score. Some composers approach this from a different perspective, incorporating a limited number of revisions that conductors can make to a completed score (e.g., no more than two additional rounds of revisions *after* the completed score is submitted).

To determine the parameters of the piece, consider the following questions about **duration** and **instrumentation**:

- "How long should the piece be?" Many composers prefer to put a range in their commissioning contracts (e.g., 5–7 minutes) rather than an exact duration.
- "What is the instrumentation for the piece?" This will likely be a specific instrumentation (e.g., chamber orchestra with a specific instrumentation provided or piano trio with electronics), but you may still have some flexibility in the piece you deliver. For example, your contract may specify an SSA choral work with or without piano.
- "How difficult should the new piece be? Are there any restrictions I should consider regarding range and divisi?" While many commissioning contracts don't specific difficulty level, some conductors may

want you to name this in the contract (e.g., Grade 4 Wind Ensemble, or SATB chorus with divisi up to eight parts). You may also discuss whether or not the piece may include one or more soloists.

To determine the **exclusivity period(s)** and **details about recording**, consider the following questions:

- "What is the exclusivity period for this piece?" Note that an exclusivity period is a timespan in which only the commissioning ensemble can perform the piece, usually up to and including the month of the premiere. If an ensemble is asking for exclusivity *after* the premiere, you may ask why: Are they planning to perform the piece again? Are they taking it on tour or hoping to record it? Longer exclusivity periods are usually granted with a specific purpose in mind. Note that even if your contract specifies a limited exclusivity period, you may choose to willingly extend that period if extenuating circumstances prevent the premiere from happening as planned (e.g., the conductor or one of the performers is unexpectedly ill and the concert is postponed).
- "Are you planning to make an audio or video recording of the concert?" As discussed in Chapter 5, a live recording of a piece can be crucial to its success. You may consider adding a clause in your contract that guarantees the commissioner will provide you with an audio and/or video recording of the concert for your non-commercial, promotional use.
- "Are you hoping to record this piece for commercial release?" Sometimes ensembles pay more for exclusive rights to record the first commercial recording of a work, while others may expect this as part of the standard commissioning contract (without an additional fee). If the commissioning ensemble wants the "right of first refusal" to a commercial recording—the option to make the first recording, which they may or may not execute—consider placing an expiration date on this right.

To determine price, consider the following questions about **budget** and **payment schedule**:

- "What is the budget for this project?" As Chapter 6 discussed, asking for a commissioner's budget first can be a more useful negotiation tactic than stating your fee outright.
- "How will the commissioning payments be divided?" and/or "What is the timeline for the commissioning payments?" Composers may use variable payment schedules for commissions, depending on the cost and

scope of a work. It is standard for a commissioner to pay half of a commission fee within thirty days of signing the contract and the second half within thirty days of delivery of the score. For a work with a larger budget and/or a work that takes several years to complete, though, a commissioner may also split the fee into more than two payments. For example, an opera commission for $100,000 might be split into the following four payments: $25,000 paid upon signing of the contract, $25,000 upon delivery of the libretto, $25,000 upon delivery of the completed score, and $25,000 upon the premiere of the work. Dividing a payment across two or more fiscal years can be favorable for an ensemble, who may be able to afford a higher fee if the cost is spread out over time.

Thinking Like an Attorney

While attorneys can certainly serve as an expert set of eyes, many creators choose to handle basic contracts, like commissions, transfer of ownership, and publishing, without formal legal consultation. You may find that you are perfectly capable of reviewing the important aspects of most contracts and only need to outsource if it's unclear what the elements are stating or requiring. Above all, as Alex Shapiro likes to say, remember that "everything is negotiable."

"I think too many people starting out are really intimidated when somebody hands them a contract," Shapiro explains. "They don't understand that that's just a starting point in the other person's favor. It's protecting their interests." But when you are approached with a contract, that's your chance to "volley back." Shapiro urges composers to consider what's in your best interest, then counter with those interests in mind.

Generally speaking, an attorney will do the same thing: they'll look at your contract with a keen eye, ensuring that your interests are protected and the contract is legally sound. If, like most of the composers interviewed, you choose to handle your contracts yourself, try "thinking like a lawyer." Here are some elements they generally look for:

Terms and Conditions

Attorneys carefully examine the terms and conditions outlined in a contract to ensure they're accurately reflecting their client's intentions and protecting their rights and interests. They assess provisions related to payment terms, delivery obligations, warranties, dispute resolution mechanisms, termination clauses, and any other relevant contractual obligations.

Legal Compliance

Attorneys scrutinize contracts to ensure compliance with applicable laws and regulations. They verify that the contract does not contain any provisions that would violate antitrust laws, intellectual property rights, consumer protection laws, or any other legal requirements specific to the subject matter or jurisdiction. (Looking for such legal requirements may be difficult for those without a law background, unless you have legal research skills from paralegal training or law school.)

Risk Assessment

Attorneys assess potential risks and liabilities associated with the contract. They identify any provisions that may expose their clients to undue risks. If these provisions exist, they'll work to mitigate them through negotiation or drafting appropriate clauses, such as indemnification, limitation of liability, or insurance requirements.

Ambiguities and Inconsistencies

Attorneys search for any ambiguities or inconsistencies within the contract that could lead to disputes or misinterpretations. They ensure that the language used is clear, unambiguous, and sufficiently detailed to avoid misunderstandings or conflicting interpretations. Generally, the more words in a clause there are, the more room for ambiguity and inconsistency.

Confidentiality and Non-Disclosure

Attorneys pay special attention to confidentiality and non-disclosure provisions to safeguard their clients' sensitive information and trade secrets. They ensure that the contract includes robust safeguards and restrictions on the use and disclosure of confidential information. There are both unilateral and bilateral non-disclosure agreements (NDAs). Bilateral agreements mean both parties agree to keep the other's confidential information private. Unilateral agreements require only one party to agree to maintain confidentiality. NDAs are typically null and void once the confidential information becomes public knowledge or information.

Enforceability and Remedies

Attorneys evaluate the enforceability of the contract and the available remedies in case of breach. They assess whether the contract contains provisions for dispute resolution, such as arbitration or litigation, and determine if the remedies provided, such as damages or the fulfillment of contractual obligations, are appropriate for their client's needs.

Overall, attorneys review contracts to protect their clients' legal rights and mitigate potential risks. Their goal is to ensure that a contract accurately reflects the parties' intentions, complies with applicable laws, and provides their client with the necessary protections and remedies in case of disputes or breaches. This contract review is something you can do yourself with enough knowledge, research, and attention to detail.

Understanding Film-Scoring Contracts

Dara Taylor suggests that if you are negotiating your first contract for film music, you should reference the "straightforward, simple" contract templates offered by and available to members of the Society of Composers & Lyricists (see the Resources section). She also recommends asking as many people as you can to assess whether a contract is fair—or "even if it's not fair, if it's typical, because sometimes those things aren't mutually exclusive."

Just as Julia Adolphe hires a lawyer when negotiating large-scale commissions, Dara Taylor has an attorney look at her studio project contracts. Her agent negotiates the terms of the deal, then sends that deal to an attorney for review. From there, the attorney will negotiate directly with the studio's legal team. In the process, Taylor's attorney checks in with her and her agent to see whether they are willing to accept the studio's counteroffer as it stands, or whether Taylor is willing to spend the time and money for the attorney to continue fighting for other terms.

Taylor notes that, on rare occasions, a film composer may begin working on a project before a contract is signed. Still, a composer should never start working before the terms of the deal are solidified. These terms may include the number of musicians to be hired, the timeline, and whether the payment is a package deal or a composing fee. "We try to get the contract signed before we start," Taylor says, but sometimes a project needs music on a compressed timeline; for example, a studio may need a final mix completed by the end of a three-week period. The occasional decision to start a project without a signed contract is largely based on a prior positive relationship working with that collaborator, Taylor says.

Identifying Red Flag Clauses

Some contractual elements immediately raise red flags for music creators, and you'll want to look out for them. One is a work-for-hire clause. The other is an indemnification clause.

Work-for-Hire Clauses

Work-for-hire clauses are some of the scariest out there. In general, these clauses stipulate that whatever you create becomes the intellectual property of the person hiring you to create that work. In essence, you are forfeiting your automatic rights to copyright protections. You no longer own your work and can collect no benefits entitled to you under US Copyright Law. In many cases, you may not even be credited as the composer and would not be entitled to make any authorship claims.

In some instances, the individual person hiring you may not even know that they are asking you to give up your copyright, since some organizations, like schools and larger corporations, may include this clause as a default in their contracts. This is certainly something you want to look out for and negotiate away, if there's room for negotiation.

It's important to note that "work-for-hire clause" is the colloquial term, but it is seldom labeled as such in a contract. Some common clause headers—if any—may include "Originality of Work," "Originality of Services," or simply "Intellectual Property." The wording could also resemble none of the above; a work-for-hire clause may lack a heading altogether. It could be embedded in a dense paragraph. To help you better identify these clauses, here's a sample from an actual contract provided by a composer who unknowingly entered into such an agreement when writing a piece for a public school. Look at the wording in bold:

CONTRACTOR agrees that all ideas, technologies, formulae, procedures, processes and methods prepared for and submitted by CONTRACTOR to the DISTRICT
in connection with the Services set forth in this AGREEMENT, shall be wholly original to CONTRACTOR and shall not be copied in whole or in part from any other
source, except that submitted to CONTRACTOR by DISTRICT as a basis for such
Services. **CONTRACTOR further agrees that all writings, materials, compositions,
recordings, teleplays, and/or video productions prepared for, written for, or
otherwise (hereinafter referred to as "Content") submitted by CONTRACTOR
to the DISTRICT and/or used in connection with the Services set forth in this
AGREEMENT, reflect the intellectual property of, and copyright interests held by
DISTRICT and shall not be copied or used in whole or in part by CONTRACTOR
without DISTRICT's express written permission. CONTRACTOR understands
and agrees that all Content produced under this AGREEMENT is the property of
DISTRICT and cannot be used without DISTRICT's express written permission.
CONTRACTOR acknowledges and agrees that DISTRICT shall have all right, title
and interest in said Content, including the right to secure and maintain the copyright, trademark and/or patent of said Content in the name of the DISTRICT.**

In other words: the DISTRICT will own your music, not you.

Work-for-hire clauses are composed in various forms and iterations, but
you should always look out for wording that implies the person hiring you
owns the work or retains the copyright of your creation. If you can't negotiate
on this point, you are always welcome to walk away from the project rather
than forfeit your copyright. In the classical concert music world, there's ample
room for negotiation on this. However, in other areas such as film scoring,
successfully striking a work-for-hire clause is highly unlikely unless it is a low-
budget film. As mentioned previously, your copyright is incredibly valuable,
tied as it is to the future adaptability and licensing potential of your work.

In very rare circumstances, you may happily agree to relinquish your
rights in a work-for-hire clause. Eric Whitacre, usually one of the strongest
advocates for keeping one's copyright, agreed to a work-for-hire clause when
he wrote his piece *Glow*. Why? Because the organization commissioning
the piece was the Walt Disney Company, and *Glow* was featured in Disney's
California Adventure winter "World of Color" water show.

"That copyright is wholly owned by Disney," Whitacre explains, "and that
was a very clear decision." For Whitacre, working with Disney was a lifelong
dream, and that justified giving up his copyright for this particular project.

When a company won't negotiate a work-for-hire clause, agreeing to these
terms may be the only way to work with that organization, no matter how
established you are in your career. In other cases, you may be asked to sign a

piece with a traditional publisher—thus transferring your copyright—as part of the terms of a commission. Work-for-hire clauses are found more often in contracts for media music, like video games and films, than they are in concert music. In any case, you won't know whether a negotiating party will agree to strike such a clause until you ask.

Work-for-Hire Clauses in Multimedia Scoring

Isaac Io Schankler points out that for video game composers, working with a AAA company—also called "Triple-A," a term for a major publisher like Nintendo or Ubisoft—often means accepting a work-for-hire contract. "The developers get the rights to your music when you compose it," Schankler says, as well as the rights to license and otherwise distribute that music. On the plus side, if smaller indie studios "can't offer you your full rate, they can say, 'Well, you get to keep the rights to your music,' and then you can put [your music] on Bandcamp [and other] streaming services and get some extra income from that." Granted, the additional licensing income might not add up to much, but Schankler notes that "it's just really mentally hard for me to sign the rights away to my creative work."

If independent video game publishers can't afford a higher rate, you can also try to negotiate a revenue share into your contract, which Schankler says rarely happens in AAA games and big-budget games. The revenue share would be a certain amount of royalties from sales of the game. "This is pretty rare these days," Schankler says, but adds:

> I got very lucky. The very first game that I composed for, the developer was very upfront: 'I can't afford to pay you very much upfront, but I will offer you this revenue share.' And it ended up being a cult hit, so I got very lucky. But that is a gamble, because if the game doesn't end up being a hit, or God forbid, sometimes the game doesn't come out at all—they never reach the end of development—then you basically get nothing. . . . But if it's a project you believe in, then that's an option.

While a revenue share is more rare, Schankler has successfully negotiated to keep the rights to all of the independent projects they've scored. They also note that, while not always part of the contract, video game composers should be aware of how their music is being used within the game:

> Is it just being used in the game? Is it being used in the marketing for the game? . . . I encourage composers to learn and understand as much as they can, even if

they're not doing it themselves, about the implementation side of video game music and what makes interactive music work, so that you have some sort of control or agency or can give people guidance about how your music is implemented in the game. That can really make or break how well it comes off in the game. It can be the best music in the world, but if it's sort of shoddily implemented and not mixed well with the rest of the game sounds, it's not going to come off as good or super professional.

Work-for-hire clauses are also standard in film music. Like Schankler, Jeff Beal notes that smaller-budget projects such as independent movies and documentaries may pay a lower rate but can often provide other incentives, like retaining your master rights or publishing rights. For the movie *Pollock*, Jeff Beal produced the score from his home studio to save costs and yet honor his artistic voice. "I recorded all the musicians and brought in the string players and real percussionists," he says. The film company retained the master rights for *Pollock*, but Beal was allowed to keep all of his publishing rights. "Because the film did so well and the score became very recognized, we very successfully licensed it to movie trailers for a few years."

If you do choose to surrender your ownership and intellectual property rights, there should be other considerations to balance or outweigh that substantial entitlement. For example, you may be able to negotiate a higher lump-sum fee, or you may be able to negotiate perpetual or fixed-term royalties for the life of the use of the property. Or, like Eric Whitacre, you may trade your copyright willingly in exchange for the fulfillment of a lifelong dream.

Indemnification

Another red flag to look out for is indemnification. An indemnification clause may be included in your contract, which generally stipulates that one person (the "indemnitor") agrees to protect another person (the "indemnitee") from certain types of harm, such as financial losses, damages, or legal costs. For example, a publishing contract clause might state something like the following: "The Composer agrees to indemnify and hold harmless the Publisher against any damage, loss, liability, injury, cost or expense."

In a musical contract, this often means that a composer might have to cover any legal issues that arise if, for example, someone claims that a piece of music you wrote infringes on their copyright. Indemnification clauses are important because they can define who is responsible if things go wrong. Whoever initiates the contract—in this case, a commissioning entity or other organization with whom you are collaborating—is more likely to include an indemnification clause that leaves you on the hook for all liabilities, rather than a reciprocal and balanced clause.

For composers, it's crucial to ensure these clauses don't place too much risk on you. Common pitfalls include agreeing to an indemnification clause that is overly broad, such as in the example mentioned earlier (i.e., "*any* damage, loss, liability, injury, cost, or expense"). If you encounter overly broad language in an indemnification clause, it's worth asking whether the scope could be narrowed to circumstances applicable to your composition.

Additionally, you might want to negotiate your responsibility to cover only direct costs or damages instead of also covering indirect or unpredictable damages. Some people have been successful in placing a monetary limit not to exceed the total value of the contract. For example, if your commission fee is $10,000, you may be able to negotiate that your total liability for indemnification is $10,000. Another negotiating point may be to explicitly state that the indemnitee cannot make any legal decisions (e.g., accepting a plea deal or pleading guilty) without your consent. This is another great reason to incorporate or form an LLC, as these entities protect your personal assets from this legal exposure.

Reading Contracts Carefully

Be prepared to speak up when you find a red flag or other confusing phrase in a contract. It is common and often necessary for contract negotiations to go through multiple drafts, and it's always better to ask for clarification than agree to terms that seem dense or unclear. Though you may be tempted to skim through a contract if you've already read through multiple previous drafts, read each successive draft thoroughly to ensure that any changes made were ones you approved.

A collaborator once inserted a clause into a late-stage draft of Melissa Dunphy's commissioning contract that could have had disastrous consequences. "I noticed a little clause in [the contract] that said that if I didn't deliver the piece on time, I was liable for unspecified administrative costs to be paid to the choir," Dunphy says. The ensemble did not specify for how much she would be liable, so if she had agreed to that clause and delivered a score late, they could theoretically have claimed that the late delivery cost them thousands of dollars. "That is very, very unusual" for a commissioning contract, Dunphy notes. While a clause in a standard commissioning contract may request repayment of a commissioning advance if a composer doesn't deliver a score, this clause about liability for late score delivery and the fact that the ensemble had inserted it into a later draft of the contract without prior agreement was a "massive, untrustworthy red flag," Dunphy says. "That's why you have to read the contract every single time."

When Contractual Agreements Go Wrong

Let's assume you've understood the basics of copyright law, had a successful round of negotiations regarding a contract offer, and entered into a contractual agreement that you find satisfactory. What happens if something goes wrong? What if there's a contractual breach? Do you need to hire a lawyer now?

First, you should always assume that people want to uphold their obligations in a contract. The failure to uphold contractual obligations is often human error—the result of an innocent mistake. Contractual breaches are commonly a result of oversight, or even good intentions. This is especially so when working with large organizations or institutions like schools.

Next, double-check your contract. Some contracts spell out what happens in a contractual dispute, while others will stipulate the jurisdiction and venue, and even require you to waive your right to take the other party to court through a process called mandatory arbitration. *Jurisdiction* refers to the legal authority of a particular court to hear a case, while *venue* specifies the location where the case will be tried.

These clauses can significantly impact a composer, as they determine the geographic location and legal system under which any disputes must be resolved. Be mindful of contracts that stipulate a jurisdiction or venue far from your home base, as this can lead to increased costs and logistical challenges. Mandatory arbitration clauses, on the other hand, require disputes to be settled through arbitration rather than in court.

While arbitration can be faster and less expensive than traditional litigation, it does have some disadvantages. Arbitration occurs outside of the court system, as it is a form of alternative dispute resolution. This means that you typically waive your right to ever take the other party to court. Unlike the court system where you generally have the right to appeal, there is no such process in arbitration. It's essential to understand that—with extremely limited exceptions—arbitration rulings are final and binding. While mandatory arbitration clauses should not be a reason to entirely walk away from a contract, you should have one key question spelled out clearly in the contract: How is the arbitrator selected? If your opposing party has the sole discretion to select an arbitrator, you are in a significant disadvantage should a contractual dispute ever arise. Your contract may also specify that an arbitrator is chosen "upon mutual agreement."

If the contract has a clause or provision specifying how disputes or suspected breaches should be remedied (or "cured," in legal terminology), you must typically follow that process first. For example, some contracts provide language for what constitutes a breach and what does not. A contract may stipulate that neither party is entitled to recover any damages unless the breaching party has a certain timeline to make the situation right (e.g., ninety days to cure upon written notification).

Still, when you believe there has been a contractual breach, it is important to take prompt action. The notion of "wait and see" is rarely a good strategy when it comes to legal obligations. Begin by carefully reviewing the contract terms to ensure your understanding of the obligations and the alleged breach. If, after your review, you are quite certain that it passes the "reasonability test" ("Would a reasonable person reach your same conclusion?"), communicate your factual concerns in writing to the other party. Cite the specific provision(s) that have potentially been violated, and express a willingness to work together to remedy the situation. Stick to facts, not feelings. Keep it brief. This is where most contract disputes resolve.

But let's say that doesn't resolve the matter. You have made multiple attempts to handle the matter through thoughtful conversation, and you are being ignored or your concern does not appear to be addressed. You have double-checked your contract, and there is no clause specifying how to handle a breach. Now it's time to send a formal demand letter.

Ideally, you want to try to resolve the matter before you get to this point. Once a demand letter is sent, relations tend to sour, and these can become difficult or impossible to repair. Only proceed to this next step if you are certain you've exhausted more casual and civil attempts and you are willing to sacrifice a relationship to gain your overall objective. If your objective is to recover a $100 payment, for example, you will want to first consider whether the relationships you might risk ending are worth $100.

Writing a Demand Letter

Demand letters sound more formal than they are, but they are the first step toward formal legal action. Writing a demand letter can be an effective way to assert your right to a resolution when you believe someone has breached a contract or committed a wrongdoing.

You don't need an attorney to send a demand letter, though it can be more intimidating for the opposing party to see you are represented by a legal professional. In the worst case, if you personally send a demand letter and it fails to result in any action or response, you can then hire an attorney for an additional demand letter. If you do choose to act on your own behalf, here are some key elements to include in that letter.

1. Introduction

Begin by clearly identifying yourself, your relationship to the recipient, and the purpose of the letter. State that you are writing a formal demand letter to address a specific issue, such as a contractual breach, nonpayment, or any other relevant matter.

2. Description of the Issue

Provide a detailed and factual account of the breach or wrongdoing. Include specific dates, events, and any relevant evidence or documentation to support your claim. Clearly explain how the other party's actions or omissions have violated the terms of the contract or caused harm, and articulate the impact or damages you have suffered as a result.

3. Request for Action

Clearly state the remedy or resolution you are seeking. This may include specific actions, such as payment of outstanding amounts, fulfillment of contractual obligations, or other corrective measures. Set a reasonable deadline for the recipient to respond or comply with your request. It is important to be clear, assertive, and professional in your tone.

4. Conclusion and Next Steps

Conclude the letter by expressing your expectation that the recipient will promptly address the issue and resolve the matter. If you are actually prepared to do so, state that you reserve the right to pursue legal remedies if a satisfactory resolution is not reached. Encourage the recipient to contact you to discuss the matter further or to propose an alternative solution if they deem it appropriate.

Deliver the copy by certified mail or other traceable proof of delivery in addition to sending it via email. In doing both, you'll ensure that it's indisputable that the person(s) who should have received the letter did indeed receive it.

In the vast majority of circumstances that escalate to involve a demand letter, this step is where the dispute will be resolved. However, you must be prepared to attempt to resolve the dispute through negotiation or alternative dispute resolution methods, such as mediation or arbitration, if stipulated in the contract. As a last resort, if a resolution cannot be reached, consult with an attorney to assess your legal options, which may include filing a lawsuit to enforce your rights and seek damages resulting from the breach.

To be clear: lawsuits are uncommon for music creators operating primarily in the classical genre. This chapter is not intended to scare you away from pursuing your creative goals. Rather, the goal is for you to enter into agreements with an awareness of the common elements mentioned in contracts, as well as the knowledge that you can always take action if your collaborator breaches their contractual obligations. With enough research and understanding, you can effectively represent yourself should things go awry. Even so, with a solid understanding of how contracts work, we're hopeful that you won't need to take that action. Many of the composers interviewed here have not yet found it necessary to hire a lawyer for help with their musical careers.

11

Accounting Fundamentals and Incorporating Your Business

Whether or not you plan to be a full-time freelance composer, mastering the business aspects of a career in music composition can be just as crucial as honing your artistic skills. This chapter delves into the intricate process of navigating the business landscape as a composer, focusing on basic accounting principles and the nuances of selecting a legal business entity type. While you'll find plenty of information relevant to building a business in composition, this is far from an all-encompassing description of accounting, incorporation, and finance. Furthermore, as noted at the beginning of this book, the information contained in this chapter is informed by laws and regulations in the United States, though many of the principles discussed can be applied universally. See the Resources section for recommended books that offer more comprehensive advice on personal finance, as well as examples of the various financial and bookkeeping software options discussed later in this chapter.

Most readers of this book will live in a capitalist society. Even if you find faults with that system, you still exist within it, and it is beyond the scope of this book to tell you how to change that system. Regardless of your personal views on capitalism, corporate culture, or taxation, consider how you and your business might benefit from the strategies discussed here. As you learn about corporate entities, it may seem as though the primary goal of incorporation is to dodge taxes and manipulate the tax system for personal gain. Keep in mind, though, that capitalism is designed to benefit businesses over individuals. While you may not be able to change capitalism through your individual choices, you can mitigate its harms through how you treat others, how you price your work, how you spend your money, and how you use your music to advocate for your personal values.

Composing a Living. Brandon Elliott and Dale Trumbore, Oxford University Press.
© Brandon Elliott and Dale Trumbore 2025. DOI: 10.1093/9780197803509.003.0012

Overview of Business Principles and Entity Types

Whether you are just starting out or looking to refine your business practices, understanding the legal and financial frameworks available to you is crucial. Here's what you can expect from this chapter:

Accounting Fundamentals

A solid grasp of accounting principles is vital for managing your composing finances. This chapter will discuss the basics of accounting methods, financial statements, and budgeting, providing you with tools and techniques to keep your finances in order. From separating personal and business expenses to leveraging accounting software, these insights will help you maintain financial health and make informed decisions.

Navigating Taxes

This section provides practical tips and strategies for navigating taxes without duplicating the detailed resources on taxation that already exist. With clarifying definitions on depreciation, amortization, and deductions, this chapter will outline common tax principles that every composer should know.

Understanding Business Entities

This chapter covers different types of business entities, including sole proprietorships, Limited Liability Companies (LLCs), and corporations. Discussions of different business entities will help you understand the role they play in your overall tax obligations. You'll also learn about their respective advantages and disadvantages, and how each can impact your personal liability and management responsibilities.

Choosing the Right Entity

Finally, this chapter will guide you to make an informed decision about which corporate entity is the best fit for your personal and business pursuits. It may be overwhelming to decide which entity is right for you, but it is vital to separate your business and personal accounts. Whether that includes forming an LLC, an S corporation, or a C corporation, know that it is easy to change your entity type later. If you decide to remain a sole proprietor, you'll still want to maintain separate business accounts and become familiar with the accounting principles below.

Accounting Basics

Many of the composers we talked with wished they had received fundamental accounting and financial literacy training while studying as composers. Many have had to acquire these skills the hard way, by learning from their mistakes. If you are daunted by accounting terms and wondering where to begin, you are not alone. While some composers hire accounting and bookkeeping professionals, many find that with the right information and software, they can manage their own books and accounts. Regardless of whether you choose to handle your bookkeeping independently or hire professional help, here are some fundamental concepts and practices with which you should be familiar.

Hired Professionals: Accountants vs. Bookkeepers

Accountants and bookkeepers provide distinct services, and it is important to note the differences between their jobs. An accountant provides strategic financial advice and prepares financial statements and tax returns, but a book-keeper handles day-to-day record keeping. As your freelance composing career grows and your finances become more complex, you may decide to hire an accountant to help with strategic financial planning and tax preparation. Similarly, if you have multiple transactions per week—incoming and outgoing payments—you may want to outsource your bookkeeping to a professional. Of the composers interviewed here, most hire accountants for help with financial advice and tax returns. Fewer hire bookkeepers, preferring to manage their own accounts.

Bookkeeping

Bookkeeping refers to the practice of regularly tracking your company's financial transactions, including incoming and outgoing payments. As you confront your own finances, you'll need to decide whether to hire a book-keeper, maintain records manually, or use accounting software. Accounting software automates these tasks and requires less hands-on management. (The Resources section includes recommendations for software and apps that can help with bookkeeping, tax preparation, and expense tracking.) Regularly update your books to ensure accuracy and ease of financial tracking. The longer you wait in between maintaining your books, the greater the risk of errors. Make it a regular routine to check in on your books on a weekly or monthly basis, depending on your overall volume of transactions.

Expense Tracking

Record Keeping

Keep detailed records of all business-related expenses. This is crucial for tax deductions and financial analysis. Maintain digital or physical records of receipts for all business-related expenses, such as travel for a performance, equipment purchases, software subscriptions, printing costs, and website maintenance fees, ensuring you can claim deductions accurately. Keep a separate business credit card and checking account to make it easier to track these expenses. Most bookkeeping software offers the option to link to these business credit or debit card purchases, logging these expenses automatically and eliminating the need to maintain receipts.

Categorizing Expenses

Organize receipts for expenses into subcategories like travel, equipment, office supplies, and so forth, to better understand where your money is going and streamline your tax deductions. As with logging receipts, bookkeeping software can make it easier to automatically sort your expenses into different categories.

Invoicing

Send invoices promptly after completing a project to ensure timely payments. Depending on your commissioning agreements, you may be required to submit an invoice alongside delivery of your scores to ensure you get paid on time. On each invoice, include necessary details such as services provided, payment terms, and due dates to avoid confusion and delays.

Financial Statements

Most bookkeeping software options will generate the following for you, negating the need to generate these reports on your own. Still, you'll want to understand what information each of these statements is showing. If you choose to incorporate your business, discussed later in this chapter, you will need the following statements in order to file your own taxes or to provide to your accountant.

Balance Sheet

A balance sheet is a snapshot of your financial position at a specific point in time. It lists assets, liabilities, and equity. For example, your balance sheet might show that you own a $2,500 computer (an asset), owe $500 in credit card balances for a recent flight purchase (a liability), and have $2,000 in equity (the difference between your assets and liabilities).

Income Statement (Profit and Loss Statement)

An income statement shows your revenues, expenses, and profits over a specific period. It helps you understand your business's profitability. As noted above, most bookkeeping software will automatically generate profit and loss statements tracking your quarterly and annual revenue. If you are not using bookkeeping software, though, it can be helpful to put together an income statement at the end of a calendar year to assess your net profit. For example, your income statement for a year might show $15,000 in commission fees, $780 in performance royalties, $2,800 in expenses for travel, and $12,980 in net profit (your total revenue minus expenses).

Budgeting

Creating a Budget

Plan your expected income and expenses by putting together a short-term and/or a long-term budget to track your income and expenses and plan for your financial future. A budget can both forecast and manage your financial resources. For example, you may want to budget for travel and tuition to attend a summer music festival. Planning ahead for this expense and allocating a set monthly savings goal based on your current income can make that expense more manageable when it arrives. Regularly compare your actual income and expenses to your budget, and make necessary adjustments.

Separating Business and Personal Finances

Separate Accounts

Regardless of whether you are a sole proprietor or have incorporated into a business entity, maintaining separate accounts for business and personal expenses is one of the simplest, yet most effective, financial actions you can take. Maintaining separate bank accounts and credit cards for business and personal use can clarify your record keeping and tax preparation. Choosing an appropriate business structure (e.g., sole proprietorship, LLC, corporation) can protect your personal assets and provide potential tax benefits. (See the section "Evaluating Corporate Entity Types" later in the chapter for more on this.)

Business Credit Cards

Composers who chose to transition to a formalized business structure remarked that they appreciated the clear separation between personal and business expenses. As mentioned above, you can further leverage this separation with separate credit cards for business and personal use.

Sydney Guillaume believes that since you necessarily spend money on your business, you might as well get some points or cash back in the process. "If I know I have a big purchase coming up," he says, "I might sign up for a new credit card if it comes with, say, a 40,000 bonus point offer. I'll be able to use those points toward a flight to attend a conference." We should note, as does Guillaume, that opening and closing credit cards does have an impact on your credit score, and pursuing points and bonus offers only makes sense if you plan to pay your balances in full each month. If you are seeking a loan, applying to rent a new space, or financing for an upcoming purchase that requires a credit check, opening a new credit card now may not be a wise idea.

Navigating Taxes

Some composers may be daunted by the potential cost of working with an accountant. However, keep in mind that hiring an accountant could save you valuable time and reduce your tax liability. This expense may not necessarily pay for itself, but the value you gain from working with a professional can be well worth the cost. Saunder Choi recognizes that hiring an accountant who truly understands his financial situation was one of the best decisions he has made. "She's very generous with offering advice, such as the benefits of incorporating," he says. Some accountants or larger accounting firms may offer a free trial meeting wherein you can ask questions and assess whether hiring that professional is right for you.

Other composers do not hire a professional accountant and instead rely on help from friends or family, or their own instincts. Abbie Betinis does her taxes with her father, and even though it takes her hours, she finds the process fascinating and learns more about her business each year:

> My dad and I do our taxes ourselves. We sit down with all the expenses from the year, and we talk them through—which expense is in which category in the business—and it's fascinating. He always says, "Do we put the expense in this category, or do we depreciate this purchase over time?" I always wonder which option is right, and my dad always says "It's not about what's right. It's about what's smartest for you."

W-2 vs. 1099-NEC Income

In considering your taxes, it's important to understand the difference between 1099-NEC income and W-2 income. Those who receive a W-2 form are considered employees. A W-2 reports wages, taxes withheld, and other employment benefits, which indicate that the employer is responsible for withholding and paying taxes.

In contrast, a 1099-NEC (nonemployee compensation) form is issued to independent contractors and freelancers for non-employee compensation, meaning the recipient is responsible for paying their own taxes, including self-employment taxes. Those who receive a 1099-NEC are considered self-employed or sole proprietors.

Many composers are paid for commissions as independent contractors, which means they are issued 1099-NEC forms. Royalties (such as performance royalty payments from PROs) are reported on another kind of 1099 form, a 1099-MISC. If you are a sole proprietor, you will need to keep track of these 1099 forms for your taxes. Composers who pay themselves a salary through their corporation will report a W-2 salary, which the section "Evaluating Corporate Entity Types," below, will discuss in greater detail.

Understanding Common Tax Principles

Know your tax obligations, including income tax, self-employment tax, and sales tax, if applicable. An accountant can help you understand the difference between these taxes, as well as your anticipated obligations for each category.

Deductions

Be aware of common deductions for composers, such as home office expenses, travel, hired personnel, and equipment. Printing scores, purchasing your website domain, and virtually anything else related to your business as a composer is likely deductible. Depending on whether you are a sole proprietor or a business entity (both discussed below), you may want to include these deductions on your taxes.

Estimated Taxes

If you are self-employed, you may want or need to make quarterly estimated tax payments. This is primarily advisable if your income is unpredictable and you want to avoid one large tax bill at the end of the year. You can make estimated tax payments to the IRS online or via a mailed check.

Depreciation and Amortization

Depreciation

Depreciation refers to the gradual deduction of the cost of tangible assets like instruments and equipment over their useful life. For example, if you purchase a $10,000 grand piano for your composing studio, you could choose to depreciate the piano over its useful life, such as ten years, deducting a portion of the cost each year. Spreading the depreciation over time could be more advantageous if you want to even out your deductions, offset future income, or ensure you're reducing tax liabilities in years when your business is expected to grow. Depreciating over time also offers flexibility in long-term tax planning, as it allows you to reserve deductions for future years when they might be more valuable.

Alternatively, tax rules like Section 179 or bonus depreciation might allow you to deduct a larger portion or even the full cost in the year of purchase. Choosing to depreciate the full value of an asset at once can be beneficial if you need immediate tax savings, particularly in a high-income year when reducing your taxable income is a priority. It also frees up cash flow that can be reinvested in your business right away.

Amortization

Amortization is similar to depreciation but applies to intangible assets like patents, copyrights, or software programs. If you purchase a software license for $1,000 that you plan to use for four years, you could amortize the cost by recording $250 in expenses each year for four years. As with any more complex tax strategy, you may want to consult an accountant about using these techniques for your own taxes.

Evaluating Corporate Entity Types

Establishing your composing business as a corporate entity can save you money on your taxes owed and limit your personal liability. Building a sustainable composing career means considering various business entity types, each with its own set of advantages and implications. In deciding which of these options is right for you at this point in your career, you will weigh factors such as taxation, liability, and operational flexibility. Below, you will find detailed descriptions of several different entity types, followed by a summary and comparison of those options in Table 11.2.

Sole Proprietorship

Everyone starts out as a sole proprietor, otherwise known as an independent contractor. In other words, to be a sole proprietor, there's no paperwork and nothing to declare, aside from filing your taxes as usual. For some composers, remaining a sole proprietor makes the most sense. In most cases, however, there can be substantial advantages to incorporating.

A sole proprietorship is the simplest form of business ownership, where the composer operates as an individual without a separate legal entity. Again, every composer starts out this way; you are one by default, unless you incorporate as another entity type. While this structure offers you simplicity and direct control, it also exposes you to unlimited personal liability for business debts and obligations. Careers in classical concert composition are usually not particularly litigious, but potential liability exposures in this field include infringement, defamation, and general contract breaches. Other sectors of composition, such as film and television, are more commonly ridden with liability matters.

Put another way: as a sole proprietor, if you are ever found liable, you as an individual—along with all of your assets, such as your house, car, or personal savings—are on the hook. You are also ineligible for the advantages available to incorporated business entities.

Advantages of sole proprietorship:

- Direct control over business decisions
- Simplicity in taxation: you file a personal tax return
- Minimal administrative requirements

Disadvantages:

- Unlimited personal liability for business debts and obligations
- Limited access to certain tax benefits and deductions available to other entity types
- Difficult to document regular employment or W-2 income if you need to qualify for a loan (auto, mortgage, etc.)

Derrick Skye started his composition career as a sole proprietor. However, when he and his wife applied for a mortgage, the lenders wouldn't accept Skye's assortment of 1099-NEC income, which was nearly 100 percent of his entire earnings as a sole proprietor. Though Skye was earning a stable income, lenders typically like to see two years of consistent W-2 or 1099-NEC income, ideally with that 1099-NEC income coming from the same source. This situation is uncommon for composers, especially when the majority of their income comes from commissions. Skye ultimately incorporated his business into an S corporation so that he would generate W-2 salaried income through composing—income that would help him qualify for a mortgage.

Many of the interviewed composers who were employed full-time in academia or arts administration were entirely comfortable remaining sole proprietors. Because these composers already have jobs with W-2 earnings, they could qualify for a loan, mortgage, or other financial instrument based on their W-2 earnings alone.

As mentioned previously, even if you choose to remain a sole proprietor, it's important to maintain separate personal and business finances.

This practice helps you keep accurate records, manage your business more effectively, and simplify tax reporting. While separating finances won't protect your personal assets from business liabilities (as sole proprietors are, again, personally liable for business debts and legal actions), keeping separate business and personal accounts is still a critical step in managing your business operations.

Several of the sole proprietor composers interviewed, especially those with a great deal of freelance income, mentioned that they have considered incorporating but are daunted by the task. Many have been delaying incorporating for years—years in which they could have benefited from the tax advantages afforded to other entity types. Even accomplished, professional composers find the task of forming a business to be confusing and challenging. With the right information and the help of an accountant or other financial professional, though, incorporating is simply a matter of deciding which entity type is right for you, then navigating the incorporation process one step at a time.

Limited Liability Company (LLC)

LLCs offer a blend of liability protection and operational flexibility, making them a popular choice for composers seeking personal asset protection without the administrative burden of corporations. LLCs are formed by filing articles of organization with the state(s) in which you conduct business. They are governed by an operating agreement that outlines ownership, management, and operational procedures.

Incorporating as an LLC is often as simple as completing one or two online forms. Do keep in mind that there is often a cost to incorporate, and some states—such as California, New York, Delaware, Massachusetts, Illinois, and Nevada—require a minimum annual tax or filing fee even if you earn no revenue for the year. Owners and members of an LLC enjoy limited liability, meaning their personal assets are shielded from business liabilities. Put another way: only your LLC and its business assets are on the hook.

By default, LLCs are typically taxed as pass-through entities, meaning profits and losses are reported on the members' individual tax returns. This avoids double taxation and is very similar to how taxes are handled as a sole proprietorship. Note that as an LLC, you also have the option to be taxed as an S corporation; to avoid confusion, we'll cover this in more detail later in the chapter.

Advantages of a Limited Liability Company:

- Limited personal liability, protecting personal assets from business debts
- Added credibility that you are a legitimate business entity
- Flexibility in management and taxation

Disadvantages:

- Some administrative requirements compared to sole proprietorship
- Taxation may be more complex than sole proprietorship
- Can incur some additional business expenses associated with maintaining a separate business, such as business liability insurance

---

Sydney Guillaume started out as a sole proprietor and, after consulting colleagues and a Certified Public Accountant, decided to form an LLC. "When you have a whole business," he says, "some conductors might take you more seriously, or realize that this is your full line of work." Asked why he chose an LLC over another entity structure, Guillaume replied, "I just chose the path of least stress." Alex Shapiro has a similar story, sharing that she transitioned from sole proprietorship while she was setting up her will. Her lawyer informed her that it would be better for her circumstances to incorporate, and she chose the LLC because it was the simplest of the options available.

Corporations: C Corporations and S Corporations

Corporations are separate legal entities formed through state registration and, similar to an LLC, they offer limited liability protection to shareholders. Corporations are formed by filing articles of incorporation with the state and are subject to various regulatory requirements, including shareholder meetings and record keeping. They are similar to LLCs, although most states do not require LLCs to hold annual meetings.

When selecting a corporation entity type, a C corporation is the default; you need to submit additional paperwork to request an S corporation designation. Both C corporations and S corporations provide liability protection, but they differ in taxation and ownership structure. Keep in mind that, just as with LLCs, some states have a minimum annual tax—regardless of your income or whether you have any profit to report—for both C and S corporations.

C Corporations

C corporations are legal entities formed through state registration, offering limited liability protection to shareholders and owners. They are subject to double taxation, where profits of the business are taxed at the corporate level and again when distributed to shareholders or employees as dividends or wages, respectively. Many composers choose to incorporate as S corporations, described in more detail below, rather than C corporations.

Advantages of a C Corporation:

- Limited personal liability for shareholders
- Potential for raising capital through the sale of stock
- More opportunities for deductions
- Can receive additional compensation via dividends

Disadvantages:

- Double taxation at the corporate and individual levels
- More complex administration and regulatory requirements

"Double taxation" may sound like your money is being thrown out the window, but the corporate tax rate is often lower than the average effective middle-class tax rate. Corporations are also taxed only on the profits of their company, after eligible expenses and losses are deducted.

Salaries paid to owners or employees in a C corporation are deductible business expenses that reduce the corporation's taxable income. This can result in lower corporate taxes, but may increase personal income taxes for the recipients. While dividends are not a deductible business expense, they are taxed at a lower rate for the individual.

If, after business expenses are deducted, C corporations have no profit to report, they may owe nothing in taxes. If this sounds unbelievable, you may be familiar with companies making headlines when they pay little to no corporate taxes through a combination of perfectly legal deductions and tax credits. As noted earlier, existing in a capitalist society can mean "playing the game" of capitalism. Learn its weaknesses, exploit them, and consider using your gains to live a benevolent life.

S Corporations

S corporations are simply C corporations (or sometimes LLCs) that have filed for a special designation by the IRS. S corporations enjoy pass-through taxation, similar to LLCs. They are also subject to specific eligibility criteria and restrictions on ownership and structure. S corporations have the option to pay non-dividend distributions, which are generally tax-free for the recipient, but there are restrictions and limitations on that tax-free income.

The owner(s) of S corporations generally must take a "reasonable" salary, taxed as W-2 income, in addition to dividends. Note that there is no single standard formula for determining what constitutes this "reasonable" salary, and your income should likely take into account factors such as the number of hours you spend working and the financial health of your company. Many individuals choose to split payments from their S corporation into 60 percent salaried income and 40 percent dividends. While this is sometimes referred to as the "60/40 Rule," there is no hard-and-fast rule for calculating how to divide your salary and your distributions. Speak to a tax professional about your specific circumstances to determine the correct ratio of salaried pay to distributions for your business.

Saunder Choi says that seeing colleagues form S corporations made him want to look into incorporating his own business, and this positive peer pressure empowered him to start a conversation with his accountant about the advantages of incorporation. For Choi, one of the biggest advantages of incorporating was "the clear separation between your personal and business assets," so that if you are sued in the future and have to close your business or pay for legal expenses with the business's investments, your personal assets will not factor into the lawsuit. "I felt like that was like one of the most important parts of the structure," Choi says.

Advantages of an S Corporation:

- Limited personal liability for shareholders
- Pass-through taxation, avoiding double taxation
- Can receive additional compensation via distributions

Disadvantages:

- Limited to 100 shareholders
- High IRS scrutiny, as it is easy to abuse the tax advantages
- Complicated regulatory requirements

S corporations have complexities that can be difficult to grasp at first but provide notable tax advantages. Several freelance composers interviewed here chose S corporation status, and almost all of them outsource their filings and regulatory requirements to tax professionals. This is in stark contrast to the many composers registered as LLCs or sole proprietors, who largely feel comfortable handling their own taxes and regulatory requirements.

Note that if you incorporate as an S corporation and must pay yourself a salary, you'll want to consider using payroll software to process those payments. Many payroll software options offer both payroll and bookkeeping services. Some platforms will also estimate and automate your estimated federal and state payroll taxes. For examples of specific payroll software options, see the Resources section. Some composers interviewed also found it helpful to ask a friend for recommendations regarding payroll and bookkeeping software as well as accountant referrals.

C Corporations versus S Corporations

If you find yourself confused about the differences between C corporations and S corporations, you are not alone. Several of the composers interviewed here feel equally as lost, and others chose one entity type over another simply because another composer colleague in their network chose the same type. If these brief summaries of different corporation types leave you with lingering questions or doubts, remember that many tax professionals will be happy to answer even the most basic questions about how to go about incorporating your business.

If you've decided that you want to move beyond a sole proprietorship and think that you would benefit more from an entity type other than an LLC, Table 11.1 demonstrates the key differences between C and S corporations. In the "Choosing Your Corporate Entity Type" section below, Table 11.2 will compare sole proprietorships, LLCs, S corporations, and C corporations, rather than more granular details of the two corporation types featured here.

Corporate Continuity: Business after Death

While it may be an uncomfortable topic, it's important to think about what happens to your entity upon your death. As a sole proprietorship, your business ends when you die. There are no formal continuity systems in place.

Table 11.1 Key Differences between C and S Corporations

	C Corporations	S Corporations
Taxation	C corporations pay taxes at the corporate tax level. Corporate taxes are a flat 21% as of publication.	S corporations are pass-through entities, meaning that you file taxes for the company on your personal tax return. The average individual federal tax rate in the United States as of publication is 24.2%.
Distributions and Dividends	C corporations can provide dividends. C corporation dividend payments are taxed at the long-term capital gains tax rate for individuals, which is generally substantially lower than personal income tax rates. At time of publication, the tax rate for long-term capital gains is 15%, as opposed to the average income tax rate of 24.2%.	S corporations can provide an additional form of compensation called a distribution. Distribution payments are generally tax-free, with rare and limited exceptions.
Salary	C corporations have no obligation to pay a salary to the owner(s). This means that the owner(s) can elect not to take a salary and instead use the company funds to cover expenses—all while enjoying a lower corporate tax rate.	S corporations are generally required to pay a "reasonable salary" to the owner(s). In other words, at least some of the revenue the company earns must be paid to the owner(s) as a salary, which will be taxed as personal income.
Scalability and Expansion	C corporations mostly benefit larger businesses. They also benefit small to mid-sized businesses that hope to scale and grow into larger businesses or strike an acquisition deal. These might appeal to composers with substantially high profiles, or composers who have multiple business segments under their umbrella (e.g., publishing, recordings, merchandise, etc.).	S corporations mostly benefit small and mid-sized businesses. There are restrictions that prevent the S corporation from expanding into larger businesses, including a limitation of shareholders and restricting ownership only to US citizens or residents. Many composers find S corporations to be the best fit for a small or mid-sized business.
Ease of Management	C corporations are a bit more complex in how they are run and managed, but they have greater potential for growth.	S corporations are easier to manage, as there are fewer shareholders involved. There are simpler tax rules, reducing the amount of annual paperwork required.

Table 11.2 Comparative Table: Key Differences between Business Entities

Entity Type	Liability	Taxation	Management Complexity	Scalability
Sole Proprietorship	Unlimited personal liability	Personal income tax	Minimal; owner manages everything	Limited; challenging to raise capital
Limited Liability Company (LLC)	Limited liability for owners	Pass-through taxation; some states have additional taxes	Moderate; requires compliance with state regulations	Moderate; more flexible for growth
S Corporation	Limited liability for shareholders	Pass-through taxation; some states have additional taxes	Higher; must adhere to specific regulations and formalities	Good; can issue shares, but with restrictions on types of shareholders
C Corporation	Limited liability for shareholders	Corporate income tax; dividends taxed separately	High; extensive record keeping, compliance, and reporting requirements	Excellent; can raise capital through issuing shares and attracting investors

With other entity types, there are systems in place to ensure continuity by default or through a few simple steps by your surviving heirs.

As an LLC, there are many options available to you to ensure continuity of your business upon your death—a practice that could financially benefit your heirs as they receive ongoing profits from your business and musical legacy. This is generally addressed in your will, trust, or estate. The LLC can generally continue to operate as a separate legal entity so long as there's a new owner to manage the company, or the new owner appoints someone to manage it.

C corporations have a rather straightforward continuity process. The C corporation continues to operate as a separate legal entity upon the owner's death. The shareholders (who could be your spouse or children, for example) would take over ownership depending on the number of shares held, and the business operations can continue without disruption.

Similar to a C corporation, ownership of an S corporation can be transferred to a shareholder. An S corporation could also be transferred according to the deceased owner's will or trust, or, if the deceased owner has left no will, according to intestacy laws. However, certain eligibility requirements would apply: the heir(s) must be US citizens or residents and consent to remain an S corporation. If the heir is an ineligible shareholder, the S corporation status is automatically terminated, and the corporation becomes a C corporation.

Choosing Your Corporate Entity Type

Your distinct personal, family, and financial circumstances will determine whether incorporating is right for you and, if so, which entity type will be most beneficial. Of the composers interviewed for this book, most preferred LLCs or S corporations, though some were content remaining sole proprietors. Again, the crucial step is not choosing the perfect entity type, but rather making the decision to separate your personal and business pursuits. If you are ready to create that separation, starting with an LLC is often ideal. Many composers begin as LLCs and find it to be the best fit for them, even years or decades later.

If the LLC no longer meets your business and financial needs, you have options. You can either dissolve your LLC and form a new entity or convert your LLC to another type. Most composers find that transitioning to an S corporation offers greater tax benefits while maintaining the simplicity of a pass-through entity. Composers with substantial fame, multiple business segments, or those looking to sell their business or seek investors may find a C corporation most suitable.

Remember, too, that your choice is not permanent: an S corporation can convert to a C corporation and vice versa. An LLC can elect to be taxed as an S corporation. You can close your business and start a new one at any time—often with just a few clicks online.

Navigating the business side of a composing career can seem overwhelming, but understanding the fundamentals of incorporating and accounting is crucial for long-term success. Selecting the right business structure can significantly impact your financial health and professional growth, and consulting with financial professionals can make a substantial difference in your journey as a composer. Whether you choose a sole proprietorship, LLC, or corporation, being well informed about your options will allow you to make strategic decisions that align with your personal circumstances, pointing you toward an organized and sustainable career. As you move forward, let these insights guide you toward a healthy financial future.

12

Preparing for Long-Term Financial Goals

Navigating the maze of corporate entities and tax advantages can be challenging, and for many composers, retirement accounts and investing principles are equally perplexing. Derrick Skye points out that even Certified Public Accountants will occasionally admit that they don't have the answers to financial questions and need to look them up. "What people need to understand is that nobody knows everything," Skye says, noting that if you feel confused or as if you don't understand, you are not alone. "When it comes to [investing and taxes], there are no dumb questions, because if you don't know and it's not clear, whose fault is that?" Not yours, according to Skye: it's the fault of the people writing opaque tax code and creating the complex rules that govern retirement accounts.

This chapter will aim to demystify and elucidate some of that complex financial information, exploring how to invest wisely and plan for retirement to ensure a financially stable future. The following does not constitute financial or investing advice, and as noted in the previous chapter, you should consider working with an expert to help you with your unique financial circumstances. Additionally, the resources at the end of this book can educate you on these topics at a deeper level.

While this chapter will provide critical information about preparing for long-term financial success, it's important to first recognize that some of these principles may feel out of reach or downright impossible, depending on your circumstances. Wealth inequality is real, and no two people have the exact same financial situation. This chapter will provide you with many investing principles relevant to musicians, but not all will apply to your specific financial situation.

In the interviews for this book, several younger composers brushed the idea of long-term financial planning and retirement to the side, while some composers nearing the end of their careers wished that they had started retirement planning sooner. When it comes to long-term financial planning, the best time to start is now. It's never too late to start or start over.

Composing a Living. Brandon Elliott and Dale Trumbore, Oxford University Press.
© Brandon Elliott and Dale Trumbore 2025. DOI: 10.1093/9780197803509.003.0013

You Control Your Finances

Composers are in the relatively unique position of having to take control of their own finances, and full-time freelance composers don't have the luxury of employer-provided retirement benefits like a traditional nine-to-five job. No matter your level of composing experience or current job situation, it's essential to take your financial future into your own hands. While the freedom and flexibility of being your own boss are appealing, a composer's income can fluctuate dramatically, and that unpredictability necessitates vigilant financial planning. You'll want to anticipate these fluctuations by budgeting conservatively and maintaining a financial cushion. You'll also want to establish both short- and long-term financial goals. Short-term financial goals may include building an emergency fund and investing in a high-yield savings account, for example, while long-term goals may include retirement planning and saving for a down payment on a home.

Below, you'll find financial strategies that can help you prioritize both short- and long-term goals. As you review the many ways to save and invest, consider leveraging a few of these options rather than sticking to just one. Earlier in this book, you learned how to diversify your skill set and income streams as a composer rather than relying on a single stream of income to meet all of your financial needs. Similarly, savvy investors usually diversify their investment portfolio, which means allocating your assets—like savings, money invested in stocks and bonds, and real estate—so that you don't have all your money invested in a single place. This strategy is vital for managing risk.

The "Buckets" Approach to Saving

As previously discussed, it is essential to your financial stability to establish an emergency fund that can cover three to six months of living expenses and be readily accessible in a savings or money market account. This fund acts as a financial safety net, ensuring you can manage unexpected expenses or cope with income gaps without resorting to high-interest debt. An emergency fund can also allow you more flexibility in which projects you accept or reject. Note that your emergency fund should *not* be invested in the stock market, where it is subject to the fluctuations of the market and can be harder to access immediately.

When it comes to saving money, consider the "buckets" approach. With many banks, you can open one savings account and label smaller sub-accounts ("buckets") wherein you can separate out money for different purposes. An emergency fund is important for those one-time sudden expenses that come up. You might prepare for unexpected expenses by creating one big emergency fund or several sub-accounts that name different kinds of expenses: "vet bills," "car repair," "birthday presents for friends and family," and so forth. Consider automatically investing a set amount of money per week, no matter how small, into these accounts.

Thomas Kotcheff notes that his mother was very good at teaching him about money, particularly the importance of saving. "I am most comfortable living my life when I am saving something every month," Kotcheff says. When he lived at home for several years, he was able to auto-invest money into savings each month. He notes that "every investment account can do an auto-pull, putting that into place." Kotcheff is always thinking about what he and his family are going to need five years in the future, so savings are a high priority. "I think anyone can put away a little bit every month, and that's so important, even if it's $10 or $20."

High-yield savings accounts (HYSAs) are excellent options for an emergency fund and short-term savings. These accounts offer higher interest rates compared to traditional savings accounts, allowing your money to grow more effectively. Standard bank savings accounts usually offer minuscule interest, so any large sums of money will be better off in a HYSA.

Certificates of Deposit (CDs)

Certificates of deposit are low-risk, short-term investments with fixed interest rates and maturity dates that often range in increments from thirty days to ten years. They offer a safe option for putting your money in savings and earning interest—often at a higher interest rate than a traditional savings account—over a specific period. These types of accounts are a great way to force yourself not to pull money from your savings accounts to cover expenses, because if you withdraw money from a CD early, you may be penalized and receive less interest. In this way, CDs can better train you to save and budget more responsibly. If you are counting on spending the money within a certain period of time, keep an eye on the end date and whether the CD has an automatic rollover or renewal. If it does, your money may be rolled over automatically into a new CD, and the interest rate may not be as beneficial as the current CD.

Debt

Avoiding Student Loan Debt

Several of the composers interviewed mentioned prioritizing paying down their student loan debt. One composer had their student loan debt forgiven under the Public Service Loan Forgiveness program, wherein people who work full-time for a government or nonprofit agency are eligible to have their debt forgiven, tax-free, after making a certain number of qualifying monthly payments.

Dale Trumbore credits her relatively early jump to working as a full-time freelance composer in part to her ability to avoid student loan debt. Though Trumbore wanted to attend New York University (NYU) as an undergraduate, her parents—both writer-editors who understood what it meant to be artists with day jobs—encouraged her to attend the University of Maryland, College Park (UMD), where Trumbore had received two scholarships that covered approximately 80 percent of her tuition. Attending NYU would have incurred close to $150,000 in student loans for Trumbore. With the money her parents and uncle had invested for her education, UMD's significant scholarship offers, and the income she made working throughout her four years as an undergraduate, Trumbore graduated from UMD debt-free.

Note that graduate students studying music composition can often find a teaching assistantship if their music theory skills, particularly those in ear-training, are very strong. If you are an undergraduate student considering an advanced degree in music composition, invest the time it takes to develop strong theory skills so that you are eligible for teaching positions when you apply for graduate school. Some schools may also offer teaching assistantships working with their resident new-music ensemble or general music classes. Overall, the teaching assistantships and stipends available to composers are sometimes large enough to cover or even exceed the full tuition amount of your graduate program.

Credit Card Debt

Debt of any kind can weigh heavily on your financial security. Credit card debt, with its high interest rates, can be particularly insidious and detrimental to your financial well-being. Consider debt consolidation or refinancing options to reduce your interest burden, and maintain a tight budget to direct extra funds toward debt reduction.

As a young composer, Sydney Guillaume says he didn't realize the impact credit cards could have:

> I was on campus at the University of Miami, and vendors would entice me to "sign up for a credit card and get a free T-shirt!" So I would sign up for them and eventually realized that actually can affect my credit. I started to be more careful with what I signed up for, and [now] I use credit cards very much like a debit card. I just focus on getting the points and I don't wait till the end of the month to pay [off a balance]. . . . I don't like to have surprises, so I always pay it off very soon after making a purchase.

With the strategy of paying off his credit cards in full every month, Guillaume enjoys the benefits of credit cards—points and airline miles, as well as building his credit—and none of the downsides.

Manage your credit wisely by paying your balances in full each month whenever possible. Many financial advisors advocate paying down cards with the highest interest rate first, but there are several different strategies for eliminating this debt. (For more suggestions, see the Resources section.)

On the plus side, building good credit can be an asset to your future. Good credit can help you access loans with favorable terms in the future, which can be beneficial for significant life expenses like a home or business investment. Additionally, responsibly spending your business expenses on a credit card that earns points or cash back is a fantastic way to reinvest into your business or to take a well-earned vacation. Selecting a credit card that offers points or cash back is a personal preference, but remember that points are a fabricated currency and could lose value far sooner than the dollar.

It is rarely, if ever, in your advantage to carry a credit card balance. To avoid exorbitant interest charges, plan to use a card only if you know you will be paying the full balance each month. With most credit cards, lucrative sign-up bonuses and earnings potential per dollar are often accompanied by a higher annual fee. Keep an eye out and do a cost-benefit analysis to see whether the amount you plan to spend will justify the annual fee.

Setting Retirement Goals

When Abbie Betinis and her husband met with a financial advisor who works in the arts, Betinis loved that advisor's definition of retirement for artists. The advisor said that for Betinis's husband, who works a standard day job, retirement looked like a more traditional 401(k) plan. For Betinis, however, retirement would likely mean making her own decisions about how much work to take on and what projects to decline. "That made a lot of sense to me," Betinis says.

Some composers aim for early retirement, while others may aspire to compose until the end of their life. Determining your retirement goals is a crucial step in ensuring your financial future. What kind of lifestyle do you envision for your golden years? Do you anticipate that you will have more, the same, or fewer expenses in retirement? Consider factors like your desired retirement age, lifestyle, and income requirements. Note that while you may be contributing to Social Security, one should not rely solely on Social Security benefits to retire comfortably.

If you have no idea how to come up with your own retirement goal, consider the commonly cited "rule of twenty-five," which suggests you should have twenty-five times your annual expenses saved for retirement. For example, if you aim to have an annual retirement income of $60,000, you would need $1.5 million saved. This is a simplified rule intended to give you a rough starting point, but individual circumstances vary drastically. If you are still feeling lost, consider reaching out to a financial advisor. If you are a member of a bank or credit union, many offer a free consultation.

Remember, time is your most valuable asset when it comes to retirement planning. The earlier you start, the more time your investments have to grow. With the power of compound interest, time can be more valuable than money. For example, setting aside $150 per month doesn't seem like it will add up to much. But at a conservative 6 percent rate of return over twenty-five years, that $150 per month can turn into a $104,854 nest egg. Don't procrastinate; begin planning for retirement as soon as you start working. Even if you are reading this book and happen to be in an older age bracket, starting today is more valuable than starting tomorrow.

Retirement Accounts

Individual Retirement Account (IRA)

Consider opening an Individual Retirement Account (IRA) as a tax-advantaged savings option for retirement. There are two main types of IRAs: Traditional and Roth.

Traditional IRA

- Tax Benefits: Contributions are tax-deductible, reducing your current taxable income.
- Tax Implications: You pay taxes when you withdraw money in retirement.
- Ideal if you expect to be in a lower tax bracket in retirement.

Roth IRA

- Tax Benefits: Contributions are made with after-tax dollars; they are not tax-deductible.
- Tax Implications: Qualified withdrawals in retirement are tax-free.
- Ideal if you expect to be in a higher tax bracket in retirement or want tax-free growth.

As of publication, approximately 41 percent of the US adult population has an IRA account. These accounts are excellent options, and many composers will be content contributing most of their retirement funds into one of these accounts. While these two IRA options are most familiar to people, there are two additional retirement account options designed specifically for self-employed business owners.

SEP IRA (Simplified Employee Pension Individual Retirement Arrangement)

- Tax Benefits: Tax-deductible contributions.
- Tax Implications: Taxed upon withdrawal in retirement.
- Ideal for self-employed individuals with variable incomes.

A SEP IRA is strikingly similar to a Traditional IRA. However, the SEP IRA allows for a much higher annual contribution limit. Jeff Beal calls the SEP IRA a "wonderful savings mechanism," noting that he began contributing to one while scoring the TV show *Monk*. At that time, he was around forty years old, starting to make more money, and increasingly thinking about his future.

A SEP IRA is great, Beal says, because the money in it grows tax free until you need it.

Solo 401(k)

> - Tax Benefits: Tax-deductible contributions with catch-up contributions for those fifty and older. Roth option available.
> - Tax Implications: Taxed upon withdrawal in retirement.
> - Ideal for self-employed individuals aiming to maximize retirement savings.

The best retirement account option for a freelance composer depends on individual circumstances and financial goals. However, considering the flexibility and potential for higher contributions, a combination of a Roth IRA and a Solo 401(k) is often an excellent choice for many freelance composers. While the Roth IRA maxes out at a certain number, the Solo 401(k) allows for significant tax-advantaged contributions.

Note that a Solo 401(k) is also sometimes referred to as a One-Participant 401(k) or a Self-Employed 401(k), but for simplicity, this book will use the term Solo 401(k). Once you have incorporated your business and have started to pay yourself a salary, you can contribute to a Solo 401(k) both as an employer (as the owner of your business) and a salaried employee of your business. This makes the Solo 401(k) a powerful tool for retirement savings.

That said, it's essential to consult with a financial advisor or tax professional to determine the most suitable retirement account based on your specific financial situation and objectives. Factors such as income level, contribution goals, and tax considerations can influence the decision. The initial cost to sit with a financial advisor may not seem worth it, but a one-time fixed consultation fee for a lifetime of maximized investing for retirement can be well worth the money.

Investing in Brokerage Accounts

Brokerage accounts allow you to invest money into stocks, bonds, mutual funds, and exchange-traded funds (ETFs) directly. You may want to prioritize investing into your emergency fund(s), funding your tax-advantaged retirement accounts, and paying down existing debt before you invest money into the stock market. But for composers who have investments in a brokerage account, the income generated from those holdings—like the dividends some stocks and ETFs pay to their shareholders—can form another kind of passive income.

As Reena Esmail has taken a long-term view to her career, she has reframed her mindset around money to prioritize residual income, wherein dividends are just as crucial to her passive income streams as her score sales and other royalties. This required a shift in Esmail's thinking, from valuing her labor in hours worked to investing in herself in ways that pay dividends. For her, this strategy includes investing in a brokerage account.

Jeff Beal credits the book *Your Money or Your Life* by Vicki Robin and Joe Dominguez with changing his approach to investing in a similar way. At the start of his career, Beal and his wife Joan, a professional singer, were new to Los Angeles and living on limited funds. *Your Money or Your Life* describes how to achieve not only wealth but financial independence. In short, to achieve financial independence, you invest until you reach a certain amount and can live off the interest and dividends of that investment without having to withdraw from the principal amount.

"It was so appealing to us," Beal says. As artists, he and his wife were interested in pursuing a lifestyle where they had more financial freedom and could take on projects that they found artistically compelling. After reading *Your Money or Your Life*, the Beals prioritized living below their means, following smart investing strategies, and becoming financially independent.

The younger you start investing and living below your means, Beal notes, the longer your investments have to grow and benefit from compound interest. The Beals began investing early in their marriage, in their mid-twenties, which allowed their investments to compound over decades. "Time is your friend in investing, so be patient," Beal says. "Putting it away, you can [invest in something] as simple as index funds."

Beal also notes that a financial crisis like a recession can be a great time to invest. "The first time you go through volatility is gut wrenching," he says, whether that's on a day-to-day basis or on a bigger scale. "Part of the key to being successful in investing is not letting those moments of extreme fear scare you out of your market." He notes that while it may feel instinctive to follow your emotions in investing—buying when a stock is going up and selling when it's low—those emotions run counter to best practices.

"There's so much psychology in investing, which is fascinating to me," Beal says. "As artists, we live by emotions, so we're emotional creatures. Part of what I had to learn being an investor was to not let emotions force me to make the wrong decision." Now Beal lives a "very charmed life," he says, but he and Joan still live below their means, as they have done all along. This lifestyle isn't about achieving any trophy possessions, Beal notes. "The real trophy is your time and your mental energy."

Capital Gains Tax

When you buy and sell assets like stocks and other funds within a brokerage, note that you'll have to pay a capital gains tax on any profitable income you make from that sale. In other words, if you've sold your assets for *less* than you originally paid, you won't owe capital gains tax on that revenue. If you have profited, though, you will owe taxes on your gains. Don't let the prospect of paying taxes on your gains stop you from investing in the stock market. You'll pay a different tax rate based on how long you've held the stock; stocks you've held for longer than a year will be taxed less than ones you've bought and sold within the span of a year. If you've sold multiple stocks during the same tax year, your total taxes owed will be determined based on your total gains or losses. These taxes are also determined based on your income, with more favorable tax rates for those who make less income.

Tax-Loss Harvesting

Tax-loss harvesting is a strategy that aims to minimize your overall tax liability. In tax-loss harvesting, if you have investments that have declined in value, you can strategically sell those underperforming assets to offset gains from other investments. By doing this, you reduce the amount of taxable gains in your portfolio. This process not only helps lower your current tax bill but also has the potential to enhance your overall investment returns. It's a way to make the most of both your winning and losing investments to keep more money in your pocket. This is a rather advanced strategy that is often best left to professionals. However, many robo-advisors offer this service.

Robo-Advisors

Robo-advisors offer an easy entry point into investing. Rather than buying individual stocks and funds through a brokerage, these automated platforms use algorithms to create and manage a diversified portfolio for you based on your financial goals and risk tolerance. They can be an excellent choice for beginners and busy professionals who want a hands-off approach to investing.

As you become more comfortable with investing in the market, you may slowly develop more interest, knowledge, and curiosity to then transfer your funds to a different brokerage where you can get granular with your investment options. (See the Resources section for a list of robo-advisors and brokerage accounts.)

529 Plans

529 plans are tax-advantaged savings accounts designed to help you or your children save for education expenses, primarily for higher education such as college tuition and related costs. These plans come in two main types: prepaid tuition plans and education savings plans. Prepaid tuition plans allow you to lock in today's tuition rates for future education, while education savings plans provide the flexibility to invest in a range of securities, potentially offering greater growth over time. Contributions to 529 plans are made with after-tax dollars, and any earnings can be withdrawn tax-free when used for qualified educational expenses. 529 plans can be a valuable tool for parents, guardians, or individuals saving for their education or that of a family member.

Real Estate Investment Trusts (REITs)

REITs allow you to invest in real estate without purchasing physical properties. Many people can hardly afford a down payment for a first home, let alone a second or third for investment purposes. REITs offer a way to access income from real estate and can provide diversification to your investment portfolio.

Peer Lending

Peer-to-peer lending platforms allow you to lend money to individuals or small businesses in exchange for interest payments. While these can provide an alternative source of income, be aware of the associated risks and diversify your peer lending investments. Some platforms provide a strong sense of altruism by allowing you to learn about who you are lending to and why. Very often, peer-to-peer lending recipients are people who have hit rock bottom and cannot obtain a traditional financial loan. By fully or partially funding a loan, you can potentially enjoy above-average returns all while helping people who need financial assistance. Like other investment instruments, you can then take the interest earnings of existing loans you've funded to fund another loan. This can further maximize your returns while growing your passive income base.

Cryptocurrencies and Non-Fungible Tokens (NFTs)

Cryptocurrencies, like Bitcoin and Ethereum, have gained popularity as alternative investments. NFTs, such as digital art and collectibles, are another speculative and high-volatility investment. Digital assets like cryptocurrency and NFTs are highly volatile, so exercise caution and consider them as a small part of your portfolio.

Estate and Long-Term Care Planning

Estate planning goes beyond creating a will. It involves naming beneficiaries for your assets and potentially establishing trusts to protect and distribute your assets according to your wishes. Consulting an attorney who specializes in estate planning can provide valuable insights.

Long-term care planning is crucial for safeguarding your future. It involves considering the costs associated with healthcare and planning for potential scenarios, including the purchase of long-term care insurance or other means to cover future healthcare expenses. Investing early in your retirement funds is not only important to cover whatever basic expenses you'll face later in life; this money will also likely fund costly healthcare expenses.

Selling Your Catalog

"The sale of your catalog is a big issue for composers," Miguel del Águila says. Particularly if you don't have heirs, he notes, you'll have to designate someone to continue managing your catalog for seventy years of protected copyright after you die. Del Águila points out that you don't want to have your music "die in a drawer," which necessitates deciding whether to sell your catalog to a publisher in exchange for a lump fee—giving up your copyright—or allowing an heir to sell your catalog in the event of your death. Other options for ensuring your music legacy include forming a trust, starting a nonprofit, or entrusting your music catalog to a university, though you ultimately have to have confidence that these entities will care for your catalog.

Jeff Beal notes that over the course of a career, your intellectual property can provide dividends that outweigh the benefit of selling your catalog for a one-time lump sum. Beal's catalog of TV and film music generates high six figures in royalties. Selling his catalog would mean giving up that passive income stream. Beal has decided that keeping his catalog—and receiving that recurring passive income—makes the most sense, and he pays taxes on his royalties as they come in. If a composer were to sell their catalog, Beal notes, they would also likely have to pay capital gains tax on the one-time income generated from that sale. The potentially large taxes owed would cut into the profit from the sale of the catalog.

Still, Beal says, if a composer were to sell their catalog and invest that amount—minus any capital gains taxes owed—that could potentially be another successful strategy. "A lot of high-profile artists have gotten some big paydays for [selling] their catalog, and I totally understand why they're doing it," he says.

Catalog acquisitions happen regularly in the music industry, though it's seldom discussed in the classical concert music space. Choosing how you want to handle your catalog when you approach retirement is as much of an emotional decision as it is a strategic one. Certain life circumstances may also force your hand. If you need the immediate lump sum of cash, a catalog acquisition deal may be your most logical option. If you have enough of a nest egg to fund your retirement and you have heirs, it may make sense for you—and your heirs—to enjoy that passive stream for decades.

Planning for retirement and investing wisely are crucial components of ensuring your financial future as a freelance composer. While the path to a comfortable retirement may be challenging, it is entirely achievable with dedication, discipline, and a well-thought-out strategy. Start early, diversify your income streams, manage your expenses, and consider consulting with a financial advisor to navigate the unique challenges of freelance life. By taking these steps, you can enjoy both your creative journey and a secure financial future.

Conclusion

Creating, Growing, and Moving Forward

Ask twenty-eight composers to define what it means to "make it" as a composer, and you'll hear just as many different definitions of success. Many of the composers interviewed named financial success as a goal: being able to support yourself and possibly your entire household with profits from commissions, royalties, and speaking or clinician gigs. Some composers cited working with professional ensembles as a marker of success, while others mentioned being able to retire on the passive income from their royalties and investments.

Some composers have rewritten their definition of success so it will apply more broadly to their lives. For them, succeeding at life means starting a family, maintaining good mental and physical health, and having a stable home life. "It can be really easy to get bogged down in how we're remembered or how many awards we win," Jocelyn Hagen says. "In the end, none of it matters. I think about my family and the projects that have been meaningful to me that I know have brought meaning to other people."

Your ambitions may look different from the ones mentioned above. They may even have evolved as a result of reading this book. As discussed in previous chapters, letting your definition of success evolve over a lifetime is healthy, especially if it de-emphasizes specific outcomes—scoring a film for a specific director, for example, or making a million dollars in score sales—and instead prioritizes systems and routines that you can control. For Abbie Betinis, money is only a small part of what brings value to her career as a composer:

> Money is definitely part of what makes up the big container of value, but it's not all of it. Other things in that container are individual for each person, but they might be artistic growth, community building, [or] changing the world. I think it has been important even for my artistic soul, but also for my own mental health, to divorce the idea of my own self-worth from the idea of how much money I'm making.

For some composers, a health concern or other shift in circumstances can necessitate reframing what success means to them. Jeff Beal notes that after

Composing a Living. Brandon Elliott and Dale Trumbore, Oxford University Press.
© Brandon Elliott and Dale Trumbore 2025. DOI: 10.1093/9780197803509.003.0014

his 2007 diagnosis of multiple sclerosis, he is more aware of the finite nature of time. He considers that recognition of impermanence to be a good thing. Composing nearly every day is integral to his mental health and well-being.

Over the course of Beal's career, his goals have evolved. "I want to be useful," he says. "I want to use my gift as long as I can to the highest level I can in the world, have that bring joy to people, and feel the joy of sharing that." That's something he is not ready to give up, though he does feel less of a need now to pursue big projects or to ascribe success to the pursuit of flashy goals. As a well-established composer, Beal's current ambitions for any project—whether that's a film score, a new opera, or a self-produced album for solo piano—are simply to do it well and "make it great." In this way, he almost feels as if he's back at the beginning of his career. He has been so lucky, he says, to have realized that he needs to stop sometimes and tell himself: "Look how lucky you are."

Beware of Shifting Goalposts and Unrealistic Expectations

As your definition evolves, be mindful of "shifting the goalpost" for yourself. This common side effect of attaining your goals involves constantly redefining success in such a way that you are never actually satisfied. Dara Taylor believes that "making it" as a composer may be a myth for exactly this reason; it's dangerously easy to turn goal setting against yourself when it comes to defining success in composition. For example, she observes that you might reach a career milestone and, instead of taking a moment to appreciate your success, you might use other goals you haven't yet achieved to prove to yourself that in fact, you still haven't "made it."

Taylor also notes that composers may feel they have achieved a certain metric of success—paying their bills with income from writing music, for example—but then their circumstances change, perhaps due to factors beyond their control. This could shatter your self-image of being a successful composer. "It's such a volatile business," she says, and as in the above examples, the concept of "making it" as a composer can actually be "detrimental to people's mental health."

While you can certainly aim high in your career, it's impossible to feel as though you are accomplishing anything worthwhile when your personal bar for success is always floating just out of reach. On the other hand, Taylor says, "you don't have to be the most successful composer in the world to have a long career, to have a good career, and to have a career that makes you feel good."

Following a Nonlinear Path

Isaac Io Schankler notes that composers sometimes expect their career to have the more-or-less straightforward path of a video game:

> I think there's this perception that a career in the arts or some other kind of career is going to have this kind of linear progression—this sort of role-playing game-like progression where you level up and fight more difficult enemies or whatever. But that rarely happens. I think, especially in the arts where there's so much volatility or arbitrariness, there are always going to be peaks and valleys and periods of feast and famine.

About ten years ago, Schankler thought they were beginning that linear trajectory, and they were disappointed when that didn't happen. For Schankler, the key to moving forward is being part of a community of kind and supportive peers. Without that community of people achieving similar and realistic ups and downs, Schankler says, "You're always going to look to and point to people who did have that linear trajectory of success. You're maybe not going to realize that that's more like the exception" than the rule. In reality, most composers have what Schankler says is a "much more interesting kind of career," with ups and downs and unexpected detours. "If you're so focused on that linear idea of success, your eyes might not be open to the other opportunities that are not in that path of your vision."

Appreciate Your Unique Journey

In one's career and even in reading this book, Miguel del Águila notes, composers should be wary of trying to follow in the path of others. Del Águila's goals were "that I was comfortable financially, I didn't have to take every single job, and I could live off my royalties," he says, and he is happy to have achieved this. "But will I tell other composers that if they don't do what I do, their career is wrong or going the wrong direction? No."

Del Águila has always written the music he wanted to hear, even living through "periods where the music of the day kept changing"—stylistic shifts that del Águila had no desire to follow. While he hesitates to prescribe advice for other composers, he recommends that you focus on your own desires and "stop trying to see what other composers do":

You are not other composers, and you're not in their world. Do whatever you want to do and do it better, because you are the best critic of yourself. . . . The most important part of your career is what you do by yourself and how you deal with what you have. I don't know what you have and what you were born with and the tools you have where you are. I think that's the most important thing composers should know: it's what they have, how they deal with it, and what they make out of it.

You May Never Feel Like You've "Made It"

While some of the composers interviewed acknowledged that they had hit certain milestones in their lives, surprisingly few felt they'd "made it." Eric Whitacre jokes that it only took him twenty years to become an "overnight success."

"I don't feel like I 'made it' at all," he says. "I still feel like I'm at the beginning of my career." Every day, Whitacre and his team continue looking toward the future, asking: "What can we do? What can we build?" He notes that from an outsider's perspective, his career may look perfect, but "it's never what it looks like from the outside, right?" His catalog doesn't reveal the full story of his composing career, he says, guessing that he has removed "probably half the music I've ever written" from that catalog. The pieces he has cut include premieres and big commissions that didn't go as well as he'd hoped.

"It looks shiny, splashy, and glamorous," Whitacre says, "but it's not like that at all." The core of a composing career, he says, is actually asking the following questions: "Are you in love with the thing you're making? And do you want to share that with the rest of the world? . . . Then, with determination, the path unfolds in its weird way, but it unfolds unflinchingly."

Sydney Guillaume's goal was always to make a full-time living as a composer and conductor. At this point in his career, Guillaume doesn't have to work to find commissions; collaborators approach him about working together. He has achieved his own definition of success. "It's interesting," he says, "because now that I'm there, I'm like, 'Now what?' It's a big question I've been asking myself." While Guillaume has very much enjoyed his career thus far, he didn't realize that achieving his vision for success would result in less time for himself. "The success also got overwhelming, and I never factored that into my goals."

Frank Ticheli notes that his career path has been like the stock market: lots of ups and downs. Even after all his successes, he says, "the honest answer is, it's never happened in my life—that feeling of 'now I've arrived.'" Ticheli's perspective on a long-term career also makes room, judiciously, for the success of other rising composers. Even if a composer were to achieve the pinnacle of success, he observes, it would be temporary:

> One hopes that it's always going to ride upward, but we also must understand that often in a composer's life, careers have a trajectory, and they may have a peak, and near the end of our life we might see it. It's the natural order of things, because new generations come along and we need to support new generations. And so the older composers might see a dip in their career, and that's nothing to be sad or ashamed about. . . . We have to make room for the next generation of composers to keep this thing going. We have to pass the torch.

Finding Fulfillment in Slow, Steady Progress

You may feel similar to the composers quoted above, realizing that commercial success alone is not enough to make a fulfilling life. Whether or not you plan to make a full-time career out of composition, you may still feel as though something is lacking. Maybe you've found great financial success with your music but realize you are traveling so much you have few hours to spend with your loved ones. Maybe you want to be writing a wider variety of pieces, but you've been pigeonholed as a "choral composer" or a "film composer" and aren't receiving commissions outside of your niche. Maybe, like Ticheli, you want to encourage the next generation of composers.

Even if finding financial success with your music is a priority, it shouldn't be the only one. A healthy career is varied and flexible. Over time, a sustainable career will see you through highlights and low points, through well-paid gigs and contract breaches, through burnout and awards and travel and imbalance.

For much of his life, Kile Smith composed while also holding down a steady day job. For Smith, being a composer was "nights and weekends," he says, "and I am actually kind of astonished from time to time at how much music I've written over the years." When his piece *Vespers* was commercially released to wide acclaim in 2008, Smith was already fifty-two years old. "People thought I was this overnight wonder, or that all of a sudden I burst onto the scene." Actually, Smith had been writing music for over thirty years, and it was those decades of experience that allowed Smith to craft *Vespers*. "I've always had to fit in composing around the edges," he says, "yet I was always doing it."

Ideally, you'll build your own path, project by project, wherein your music sustains you in multiple facets of your life. Through careful financial planning, you can amass wealth that grants you dividends and retirement income as well as free time: days in which you can pursue whatever passions compel you, musical or not. Through creating music, you can find financial gains but also artistic freedom—room to explore and grow emotionally through your art.

Morten Lauridsen finds joy in knowing how well his music has been received, yes, but also in how music has allowed him to explore universal themes of love and loss:

> I am honored by the overwhelming worldwide response to my music. I must note that this was evident only after I had turned 50 years of age, when several of my works became performed throughout the world and a series of my recordings garnered Grammy nominations. At that time listeners discovered my earlier works, which then added immensely to sales of scores in the millions and hundreds of recordings. I simply sought throughout my career to compose music that was solidly crafted on texts by acclaimed poets that spoke to the listener on universal subjects encompassing us as humans, principally those involving love gained and lost, grief and departure of loved ones, nature and spirituality. That these works have been deeply received and responded to by performers and listeners is a source of profound joy and gratification for me.

Pursuing your music career requires a holistic approach: you are not just the creator of your music. You are the sum of your art, your relationships, and your contributions to the world as a human being.

Redefining Success

Alex Shapiro's singular concept of "making it" is this: "Do I have a happy life when I open my eyes in the morning? Am I where I want to be?" When you are happy, she notes, you are driven naturally to keep doing the thing that makes you happy. "For the most part, we're all doing this not because we're going to make millions and millions of dollars, but because we're passionate about making art. How beautiful is that?"

Every interview for this book started as a dialogue about money and turned into a conversation about relationships. Want to build passive income? You'll need a community that values your work, and you build that community one person at a time. Want more commissions? Build your community by focusing on one relationship at a time and asking how you can serve that community. If you meaningfully contribute to a community, that community will support you in turn. Fans of your music will tell their friends to listen to it. Conductors will program it, and other conductors will hear your work.

"We earn our place," Shawn Kirchner says. "We earn the respect of our peers and our colleagues by putting in the effort over the years. By a track record. By piece after piece after piece. By showing consistency. By being reliable to people. By them finding our music meaningful and moving and musically interesting and worth their time. That is how you build a career."

Some of your collaborators will become your closest friends. Those relationships can benefit your income, of course, as these collaborators commission you to work for them and purchase your scores. They can also lead to lifelong friendships for which you couldn't possibly assign a monetary value—no number would be high enough.

There's no single blend of knowledge of relationship building, craft, imagination, and financial savvy that makes up a composing career, and no one path to success. Certain strategies do apply to most composers, and they're the ones already described in this book: Cultivate a network of people whom you respect as human beings as well as collaborators. Invest in yourself and your relationships, ascribing value to non-monetary exchanges as well as monetary ones. Prioritize intentional systems and daily routines over rigid goal setting. Diversify your skill set and your income streams.

In the end, though, it's up to you to define what success could look like for you. It's up to you to identify the systems that could put that success in place and then to build your path brick by brick. It's never too late to change direction, and it's okay to change your mind about your destination. It's even okay if you ultimately decide a career in composition isn't for you; whatever you do next, you will have the tools to build a sustainable, creative life.

What matters most is that you nurture solid relationships and remain adaptable in the face of change. This career is an inherently unstable one. Keep creating, keep growing, and keep moving forward toward your north star. Your journey as a composer is uniquely yours, and your success—however it is defined—will be as distinctive as the music you write.

Resources

Inclusion on this list, particularly regarding financial services, does not imply an endorsement on behalf of the authors.

Chapter 1: Starting to Start

Professional Organizations

American Choral Directors Association (ACDA) (https://acda.org/)*
Chamber Music America (https://chambermusicamerica.org/)
Chorus America (https://chorusamerica.org/)
College Band Directors National Association (CBDNA) (https://www.cbdna.org/)*
League of American Orchestras (https://americanorchestras.org/)
Opera America (https://www.operaamerica.org/)
The Society of Composers & Lyricists (https://thescl.com/)
Note that under the umbrella of these organizations, there are also regional chapters, which provide multiple points of entry for composers for a single membership fee.

Recommended Reading: Concert Composition

Baumgardner, Astrid. 2019. *How Creatives Can Thrive in the 21st Century*. Indie Books International.

Beeching, Angela Myles. 2020. *Beyond Talent: Creating a Successful Career in Music*. 3rd ed. Oxford University Press.

Cutler, David. 2025. *The Savvy Musician 2.0*. 2nd ed. Oxford University Press.

Nytch, Jeffrey. 2018. *The Entrepreneurial Muse: Inspiring Your Career in Classical Music*. Oxford University Press.

Timmons, Jill. 2023. *The Musician's Journey*. 2nd ed. Oxford University Press.

Recommended Reading: Multimedia Composition

Brown, Bill. 2024. *Working as a Film Composer: The Art and Business of Composing for Film, TV and Games*. Softwood Books.

Davis, Richard. 2010. *Complete Guide to Film Scoring: The Art and Business of Writing Music for Movies and TV*. 2nd ed. Berklee Press.

Karlin, Fred. 2004. *On the Track: A Guide to Contemporary Film Scoring*. 2nd ed. Routledge.

Melin, Steven. 2019. *Family-First Composer: Proven Path to Escape 9–5 and Support Your Family Composing Music for Film, TV, & Video Games*. Independently published.

Phillips, Winifred. 2017. *A Composer's Guide to Game Music*. The MIT Press.

Thomas, Chance. 2015. *Composing Music for Games: The Art, Technology and Business of Video Game Scoring*. Routledge.

Chapter 2: Building Relationships

Customer Relationship Management (CRM) Apps and Softwares

Cloze (https://www.cloze.com/)
Covve (https://covve.com/)
Dex (https://getdex.com/)
HoneyBook (https://www.honeybook.com/)
Monday CRM (https://monday.com/crm)

Conferences

American Choral Directors National Conference (https://acda.org/)
The Composer's Guide to Choral Conferences (https://www.daletrumbore.com/conferences)
Chamber Music America Conference (https://chambermusicamerica.org/)
Chorus America Conference (https://chorusamerica.org/annual-conference)
Game Developers Conference (https://gdconf.com/)
The Midwest Clinic, International Band and Orchestra Conference (https://www.midwestclinic.org/)

Chapter 3: Cultivating a Successful Mindset

Recommended Reading

Gannon, Emma. 2023. *The Success Myth: The Inspirational Guide to Defining Success on Your Own Terms.* Transworld Digital.
Trumbore, Dale. 2019. *Staying Composed: Overcoming Anxiety and Self-Doubt within a Creative Life.* Independently published.

Chapter 4: Goals and Economics: A Strategic Balance

Recommended Additional Reading

Clear, James. 2018. *Atomic Habits.* Avery.
Dominguez, Joe, and Vicki Robin. 2018. *Your Money or Your Life.* Rev. ed. Penguin Books.
Luttrull, Elaine Grogan. 2013. *Arts and Numbers: A Financial Guide for Artists, Writers, Performers, and Other Members of the Creative Class.* Agate B2.
Sethi, Ramit. 2019. *I Will Teach You to Be Rich.* 2nd ed. Workman.
Shen, Kristy, and Bryce Leung. 2019. *Quit Like a Millionaire.* TarcherPerigee.
Wheelan, Charles. 2019. *Naked Economics: Undressing the Dismal Science.* 3rd ed. W. W. Norton.

Chapter 5: Establishing a Strong Foundation

Distribution Options for Self-Releasing Recordings

CD Baby (https://cdbaby.com/)
DistroKid (https://distrokid.com/)
TuneCore (https://www.tunecore.com/)

Free Resources: Sample Libraries, Plug-Ins, and Editing Software

Audacity (https://www.audacityteam.org/) Free audio-editing software.

iZotope (https://www.izotope.com/en/products/free-audio-plug-ins.html) Free plug-ins and tutorials.

Native Instruments (https://www.native-instruments.com/en/catalog/free/) Free sound libraries within the Native Instruments catalog.

Project SAM (https://projectsam.com/series/the-free-orchestra) Free sample library.

Spitfire Audio (https://www.spitfireaudio.com/) Free and paid sample libraries.

ValhallaSupermassive (https://valhalladsp.com/shop/reverb/valhalla-supermassive/) Free and paid plug-ins.

Free Resources: Perusal Scores

Boosey & Hawkes Online Scores (https://www.boosey.com/cr/perusals/). Provides access to over two thousand perusal scores in the Boosey & Hawkes catalog. Free access with registration.

International Music Score Library Project (IMSLP) Petrucci Music Library (https://imslp.org/). Free access to over 700,000 scores, many of them in the public domain.

University of California, Los Angeles (UCLA) Contemporary Music Score Collection (https://www.library.ucla.edu/collections/explore/contemporary-music-score-collection/). Contemporary music library where scores may be viewed and downloaded for free.

Free Resources: Writing for Various Instruments, with Extended Techniques

Instrument Studies for Eyes and Ears (https://isfee.music.indiana.edu/) (Indiana University, Jacobs School of Music). This site provides detailed explanations of instrument ranges, with example scores and videos.

Shaken Not Stuttered (https://www.shakennotstuttered.com/). An online resource created by Anne Leilehua Lanzilotti to demonstrate the extended techniques for strings, with score and audio examples excerpted from various compositions.

Recommended Reading

Burgess, Richard James. 2013. *The Art of Music Production: The Theory and Practice*. 4th ed. Oxford University Press.

Time Management: Software and Apps

Any.Do (https://www.any.do)

Clockify (https://clockify.me/)

Forest (https://www.forestapp.cc/)

Todoist (https://todoist.com/)

Luminate (SoundScan Reporting) (https://luminatedata.com/)

Chapter 6: Pricing Your Work

Nonprofit Research

IRS Tax Exempt Organization Search (https://www.irs.gov/charities-non-profits/search-for-tax-exempt-organizations)

GuideStar (https://www.guidestar.org/search)

Pricing Guides

Composer Commission Pay Survey (https://lorettanotareschi.com/composer-commission-pay-survey/)

NewMusic USA Pricing Calculator (https://newmusicusa.org/nmbx/commissioning-fees-calculator/)

GameSoundCon: Survey of Game Audio Industry Creator Salaries (https://www.gamesound con.com/survey)

Recommended Reading

Wixen, Randall D. 2024. *The Plain & Simple Guide to Music Publishing*. 5th ed. Hal Leonard.

Selected Sheet Music Distributors (Digital and/or Printed)

Graphite Marketplace (https://graphitepublishing.com/)
MusicSpoke (https://musicspoke.com/)
J.W. Pepper's MyScore (https://www.jwpepper.com/myscore)
Murphy Music Press (https://murphymusicpress.com/)

Chapter 7: Diversifying Income Streams

US Performing Rights Organizations (PROs)

ASCAP (https://www.ascap.com/)
BMI (https://www.bmi.com/)
SESAC (https://www.sesac.com/)

Collective Rights Management Organizations

SoundExchange (https://www.soundexchange.com/)

Digital Service Provider (DSP) Mechanical Fee Collections

Mechanical Licensing Collective (MLC) (https://www.themlc.com/)

Rights Organization for Composers of Church Music

OneLicense (https://www.onelicense.net/)

Recommended Additional Reading

Forrest, Dan, with Jake Runestad. "The Business of Composing, Part 1: Commissions and Publishing," *Choral Journal*, March–April 2023, 24.
Forrest, Dan, with Jake Runestad. "The Business of Composing, Part 2: Licensing," *Choral Journal*, March–April 2023, 34.

Chapter 8: Assembling Your Team

General Automation Tools and Database Management: Software and Apps

Airtable (https://www.airtable.com/)
Notion (https://www.notion.so/)
Zapier (https://zapier.com/)
Zoho Flow (https://www.zoho.com/flow/)

Social Media Scheduling and Management: Software and Apps

Loomly (https://www.loomly.com/)
Hootsuite (https://www.hootsuite.com/)
SproutSocial (https://sproutsocial.com/)
Planable (https://planable.io/)
CoSchedule (https://coschedule.com/)

Project Management: Software

Trello (https://trello.com/)
Jira (https://www.atlassian.com/software/jira)
Asana (https://asana.com/)
Monday (https://monday.com/)

Financial Management: Software

QuickBooks (https://quickbooks.intuit.com/)
Wave (https://www.waveapps.com/)
Xero (https://www.xero.com/us/)
FreshBooks (https://www.freshbooks.com/)

Chapter 9: Transitioning to 100 Percent Freelance Composing

Recommended Reading

Berkun, Scott. 2009. *Confessions of a Public Speaker*. O'Reilly Media.
Koch, Deborah S. 2009. *How to Say It: Grantwriting: Write Proposals That Grantmakers Want to Fund*. Prentice Hall.
Larsen, Gail. 2009. *Transformational Speaking: If You Want to Change the World, Tell a Better Story*. Clarkson Potter/Ten Speed.

Chapter 10: Navigating Copyright, Contracts, and Legal Basics

Further Reading

Halloran, Mark. 2017. *The Musician's Business and Legal Guide*. Routledge.
Moser, David J. 2011. *Music Copyright Law*. Cengage Learning PTR.

Examples of Film-Scoring Contracts

The Society of Composers & Lyricists (https://thescl.com/contract-templates/)
Legal Resources
LegalZoom (https://www.legalzoom.com/)

United States Copyright Laws

Title 17 of the United States Code (Copyright Laws) (https://www.copyright.gov/title17/)

Chapter 11: Accounting Fundamentals and Incorporating Your Business

Expense Tracking: Apps

Several of the bookkeeping softwares listed above, such as Wave and Quickbooks, have smartphone apps where you can digitally upload your receipts for better expense tracking, or you may choose a standalone expense tracking application:
Evernote (https://evernote.com/) (Scan & Convert Image to PDF)
Expensify (https://www.expensify.com/) (Expense Management)

Payroll and/or Bookkeeping: Software

Gusto (https://gusto.com/) (Bookkeeping and Payroll)

Quickbooks (https://quickbooks.intuit.com/) (Bookkeeping) or QuickBooks Payroll (https://
   quickbooks.intuit.com/payroll/) (Payroll)
Wave (https://www.waveapps.com/) (Bookkeeping and Payroll)
CreditKarma (https://www.creditkarma.com/) (Free Credit Score monitoring)

Free Business Mentoring and Resources

SCORE (https://www.score.org/)

Chapter 12: Preparing for Long-Term Financial Goals

Brokerage Accounts

Fidelity (https://www.fidelity.com/)
Charles Schwab (https://www.schwab.com/)
Vanguard (https://investor.vanguard.com/home)
E*Trade (https://us.etrade.com/home)
J.P. Morgan (https://www.jpmorgan.com/global)

Robo-Advisors

Betterment (https://www.betterment.com/)
Wealthfront (https://www.wealthfront.com/)

Peer Lending

Prosper (https://www.prosper.com/)
Kiva (https://www.kiva.org/)

Acknowledgments

Tremendous thanks to the composers featured in this book, who generously offered their time and insight: Julia Adolphe, Miguel del Águila, Juhi Bansal, Jeff Beal, Abbie Betinis, Saunder Choi, Melissa Dunphy, Reena Esmail, Sydney Guillaume, Jocelyn Hagen, Jennifer Jolley, Molly Joyce, Shawn Kirchner, Morten Lauridsen, Thomas Kotcheff, Angélica Negrón, Shara Nova, Zanaida Stewart Robles, Jake Runestad, Isaac Io Schankler, Alex Shapiro, Derrick Skye, Kile Smith, Timothy C. Takach, Dara Taylor, Frank Ticheli, Mari Esabel Valverde, and Eric Whitacre. Thank you, too, to Dominick DiOrio, Michael Gilbertson, and Emma O'Halloran.

Thank you to our immensely helpful beta readers: Ayo Awosika, Nick Benavides, Marcus Carline, Kai-Young Chan, Colleen Chester, Grace Coberly, Ian Coleman, Brandon Di Noto, Alex Grabarchuk, Christian Guebert, Brian Head, Rex Isenberg, Cindy Kane, Laura Kramer, Marybeth Kurnat, Tara Mack, Hannah McMeans, Rich Messenger, Kyle Pederson, Stacey Philipps, Nathan Scalise, Scott Senko, Rachel Lanik Whelan, and Deanna Witkowski.

Thank you to Dale Warland for putting us in touch all those years ago and for supporting us in all our creative endeavors.

Thank you to Justin Thai and Jake Morgan for assisting with interview transcripts.

Thank you to Michelle Chen, Rada Radojicic, and Timothy DeWerff for shepherding this book to publication.

From Dale: Love and thanks to Cindy, Harry, Doug, Lisa, Kieran, and Emilia. Thank you Luke for being a wonderful, supportive partner in all things (including the property taxes).

From Brandon: With love and gratitude for Colleen, Chris, Mike, Karen, Seth, Michael, my Choral Arts Initiative family, and all my students—current and past.

About the Authors

Dr. Brandon Elliott is an influential conductor, educator, and consultant dedicated to empowering artists to thrive at the intersection of music, business, and creative growth. As Founder and Artistic Director of Choral Arts Initiative, Brandon has shaped an award-winning new music ensemble that champions contemporary choral works, commissioning over twenty-five works, premiering more than 150 works, and producing three Billboard-charting albums. His leadership has positioned Choral Arts Initiative as a leading voice in innovative choral performance and artistic development, garnering accolades such as the ASCAP/Chorus America Award for Adventurous Programming and the Louis Botto Award for Innovation and Entrepreneurship.

In academia, Brandon serves as Professor of Music and Director of Choral and Vocal Studies at Saddleback College and as Lecturer in Music Education at California State University, Fullerton, where he guides emerging musicians with a focus on resilience, artistry, and entrepreneurship. His dedication to lifelong learning and comprehensive music education has been recognized by the Recording Academy, where he was honored as a GRAMMY Music Educator Award semifinalist.

Brandon's consultancy extends into the broader entertainment industry, advising on music rights, artist management, and strategic growth for creatives and organizations. His expertise in contract negotiation, leadership development, and inclusion initiatives has made him a sought-after consultant and industry commentator, featured in *US News & World Report*, *Lifewire*, and other major outlets. A trusted mentor and visionary in the arts, Brandon is committed to fostering sustainable artistic careers and shares insights through industry publications, podcasts, speaking engagements, and conferences. Learn more at brandon-elliott.com.

Dale Trumbore is a Los Angeles–based composer and writer whose music has been called "devastatingly beautiful" (*Washington Post*) and praised for its "soaring melodies and beguiling harmonies deployed with finesse" (*New York Times*). Trumbore is passionate about setting to music poems, prose, and found text by living writers. She has written extensively about working through creative blocks and establishing a career in music in essays for *21CM*,

Cantate Magazine, Center for New Music, and *NewMusicBox*. Her first book, *Staying Composed: Overcoming Anxiety and Self-Doubt within a Creative Life*, was hailed by writer Angela Myles Beeching as a "treasure trove of practical strategies for moving your artistic career forward." Trumbore also writes poetry and fiction, with work published in *F(r)iction, New Delta Review, PRISM International, Southern Indiana Review*, and other literary journals.

Trumbore's compositions have been performed widely in the United States and internationally by the Atlanta Master Chorale, Central West Ballet, Chicago Symphony's MusicNOW ensemble, Conspirare and the Miró Quartet, Los Angeles Master Chorale, Pasadena Symphony, Phoenix Chorale, and Seraphic Fire, among others. Her music is published through Boosey & Hawkes and G. Schirmer and distributed through Graphite Marketplace. Learn more about Trumbore's music and writing at daletrumbore.com.

Index

For the benefit of digital users, indexed terms that span two pages (e.g., 52–53) may, on occasion, appear on only one of those pages.